TEACHING ELECTRONIC INFORMATION LITERACY

A How-To-Do-It Manual

Edited by
Donald A. Barclay

**HOW-TO-DO-IT MANUALS
FOR LIBRARIANS**

NUMBER 53

NEAL-SCHUMAN PUBLISHERS, INC.
New York, London

Published by Neal-Schuman Publishers, Inc.
100 Varick Street
New York, NY 10013

Printed and bound in the United States of America.

Library of Congress Cataloging-in-Publication Data

Teaching electronic : information literacy : a how-to-do-it manual /
  [edited by] Donald A. Barclay.
      p. cm. — (How-to-do-it manuals for librarians ; no. 53)
  Includes bibliographical references and index.
  ISBN 1-55570-186-8 (alk. paper)
  1. Database searching—Study and teaching. I. Barclay, Donald A.
II. Series: How-to-do-it manuals for libraries ; no. 53.
Z699.T34   1995
025.04'07—dc20   95–31401

CONTENTS

INTRODUCTION

The intended audience for *Teaching Electronic Information Literacy* is working librarians, teachers, and trainers who are already somewhat familiar with accessing and using electronic information resources but who find themselves asking the hottest information question of the 1990s—"How do I teach this stuff?" It is clear from the number of megabytes spilled on this question that the answer is complex. To try to strip away some of the complexity, this book does not concern itself with the important issues of who should teach electronic information literacy or what makes a person an electronic information literate. These questions can be answered elsewhere by others. It is the purpose of this book to guide those in the trenches so they can get on with the important business of teaching people to access and use electronic information.

In approach this book tries to strike a balance between the specific and the general. In a volatile information world—where hardware, software, and terminology change too fast for anyone to keep up—the editor and contributors wanted to avoid making this book into a guide to using specific electronic information tools that might quickly disappear or become dated. For example, as this book goes to press Mosaic software is all the rage among Internet insiders, with a commercial product called Netscape getting some press as heir apparent. By the time you read this, these products may have disappeared and been replaced by even newer innovations—making obsolete any book that attempted to serve as a guide to Mosaic or Netscape. On the other hand, this book is not meant to be just a philosophical ramble on the nature of electronic information, but it is trying to achieve a balance by looking at electronic information universals—including introducing new users to Internet culture, designing effective written guides, and coordinating a successful workshop—from a practical, how-to-do-it point of view. Most of all, it is hoped that you will find this book useful as you help others to become full participants in the Information Society.

1 META-LEARNING FOR PROFESSIONAL DEVELOPMENT

Deborah Fink
University of Colorado at Boulder Libraries
with
Abigail Loomis
University of Wisconsin-Madison Libraries

Just as telecommunications have made the planet a global village, so they have made electronic information resources a global library, where library catalogs are one type of node. As the larger context within which librarians function continues to evolve, every aspect of who we are and what we do is open to question, including: how we serve, whom we serve, sources of information, access to information, organizational structure, workplace culture, work flow, and the very "body of knowledge" that defines our field. The foundation of library service, i.e., the collection and access, remains stable, however. Information in various formats must still be collected, organized, and preserved; and that information must still be identified and located by users. This chapter suggests an approach for developing a personal professional development plan for working in the electronic library and teaching electronic information literacy.

The availability of hardware and software has not *fundamentally* changed the function or even appearance of libraries. However, it *has* dramatically changed the role of librarians. We are no longer experts—masters and practitioners of a known body of knowledge. We are no longer experienced guides to a familiar terrain. We must be—can only be—explorers, scouts, and pathfinders, navigating unbounded, evolving sources of information to map the way for users who are now fellow searchers. As computerized information access takes hold in the classroom, office, and home, the distinction between expert and lay person dissolves. New electronic resources are available so widely and frequently that users have more exposure to them, and librarians often lack the time and opportunity to master them before assisting users. Librarians, at this juncture, can only stay a little ahead of the lay searcher and concentrate instead on honing traditional skill at making and disseminating maps.

The mandate to keep changing the way we function as librarians is a challenge, in part, because of the very human inclination to continue doing what we know we can do well. We are reluctant to risk making mistakes or looking incompetent or foolish; we resist being in the learner mode (particularly in front of our own students!). We keep on doing what we already do rather than embrace the challenge of learning new tasks or approaches. But we must accept learning as a new constant in our profession and learn how to learn. We must make professional development a routine component of our work. Our institutional organizational cultures must accommodate what this requires, i.e., as a profession to handle our housekeeping more effectively and efficiently in order to focus on continuous professional development.

Professional development no longer can be a reward, interruption, interlude, or occasional boost; it must be integrated into our admittedly already overloaded daily agenda of responsibilities. This is especially critical for the teaching librarian who must keep up with *and* create curricula for the latest developments. It is also especially beneficial for the teaching librarian because our own mastering of new material infuses our teaching with the excitement of learning, and the best way to instill this in our students is by example.

SIX STAGES IN THE CREATION OF A PERSONAL PROFESSIONAL DEVELOPMENT PLAN

1. Establishing a professional development goal and objectives en route to that goal.
2. Identifying your personal learning style.
3. Surveying the subject or skill to be learned.
4. Creating a plan.
5. Implementing and monitoring the plan.
6. Integrating professional development into your professional life.

1. ESTABLISHING A PROFESSIONAL DEVELOPMENT GOAL AND OBJECTIVES EN ROUTE TO THAT GOAL

The decision to engage in professional development—or on-the-job education—will likely result from a perceived gap in working knowledge. Such gaps are unavoidable given the current pace of technological advancement. They are as probable for the recent graduate who is confronted with situations not covered sufficiently in library school as for the seasoned veteran who is working with resources unheard of in library school. A perceived gap is very typical in mid-career when you have the opportunity or need to assume some new responsibility or a new position, or when significant changes occur in the workplace, such as the implementation of a new automation system or organizational structure. You may engage in professional development with great enthusiasm, feeling challenged and excited about the opportunity, or, although convinced of the importance, you may experience great reluctance or resistance. Whatever the circumstances and internal response, the first step is to articulate the need and a goal.

State the need as precisely as possible, coupled with an outcome and goal. The need becomes the rationale for your professional development project, and the goal provides motivation and parameters.

For example, I need to:

- learn to navigate the Internet in order to keep up with important developments in my profession.
- familiarize myself with the Wilson CD-ROMs in order to develop guides for their use.
- become grounded in learning theory and bibliographic instruction in order to develop an orientation program for freshmen.
- study instructional design in order to create a multimedia library tour.
- round out my understanding of electronic technology in order to update a credit library course.
- learn design and production principles in order to create better visual aids for teaching electronic technology.
- master telecommunications software in order to train others in my library.
- master desktop publishing in order to upgrade and streamline our publications program.
- further my understanding of management theory in order to be a better supervisor.
- deepen my knowledge of cataloging practice in order to perform my job better.
- study the computer-user interface in order to select and design the best possible automation system.

It is crucial to acknowledge personally that your goal is a legitimate, appropriate, and necessary professional responsibility. Only you can determine how to value and sustain commitment to your goal. When possible, it is helpful also organizationally to establish the goal, so that, for example, your institution provides for including such a goal in an annual goal-setting or assessment procedure. As professionals, librarians uphold a commitment to a number of basic responsibilities, including adhering to widely agreed-upon standards and ethics and making contributions to the profession. Ongoing professional development is no less fundamental.

2. IDENTIFYING YOUR PERSONAL LEARNING STYLE

Identify your personal learning style and, if desired, learn more about learning styles in general.

There are many models that classify approaches to learning, from simple bipolar designations to complex multidimensional systems. Some researchers, for example, maintain that the many different types of style may simply be categorized as splitting or lumping. Splitters, or left-brain types, like to break things down into component parts or categories; lumpers, or right-brain dominants, are more holistic and relational. A complex multidimensional model is the Myers-Briggs Type Indicator that provides scores along four dichotomous scales: extraversion versus introversion, sensing versus intuition, thinking versus feeling, and judging versus perception. Learning styles have been correlated to the resulting 16 Myers-Briggs personality types.

One of the disadvantages of using a predetermined model to identify your style is the likelihood of defining yourself within a box that doesn't include some important aspects of your approach, creates some disproportionate focus, or just doesn't fit. As experienced learners, you have each developed a style of learning, which not only serves you well, but also could be useful if modeled for less practiced learners still learning how to learn. It is easy to determine your own unique approach based on a personal assessment of a learning experience. Opportunities to apply standardized instruments may reveal additional facets of your approach to learning that can be woven together with the results of your own appraisal if desired.

Style indicators are fascinating not only for what they reveal about yourself, but also for what they tell you about how people differ and how to relate more effectively to people who *are* different. One of the advantages of becoming familiar with one or more learning style models and applying them to teaching is an increased awareness of and sensitivity to the potential range of learning skills and preferences in the classroom. Research indicates that teachers teach the way they prefer to learn and are more responsive to and appreciative of students who are closest to their own type. Those students who are most like their teacher, therefore, may be pedagogically advantaged in both the way their learning environment is structured as well as the way they are reinforced. When you teach to an entire spectrum of styles, each student has the opportunity to learn under preferred conditions and to be challenged in areas that require surpassing limits and thereby developing new skills.

Teaching librarians who wish to maximize their professional development and apply the results to the classroom, would do well to become familiar with any of the available learning style models (see References) and to identify their own personal learning style (see "Meta-Learning" at the end of this chapter).

3. SURVEYING THE SUBJECT OR SKILL TO BE LEARNED

Survey the subject or skill to be learned by talking to others, using electronic discussion lists, perusing some literature, or attending workshops or conferences.

Now that you have a picture of how you learn best, you need to begin building a picture of the subject area to be learned. Develop a sense of the scope of the topic or skill to be pursued and potential avenues for learning about it. Perhaps you have been saving articles and references about the subject for some time and can start by sorting your own file. You also can talk to others, use discussion lists, peruse some literature, or attend workshops and conferences. The approach you take will be determined by your learning style preference.

Some examples are: By chatting with colleagues, you may learn that others have already become skilled users of the Internet and love to demonstrate their facility. In perusing educational journals, you could identify the current issues in learning theory. You may be able to determine what others think about Total Quality Management on a management Listserv and begin posing some questions and requesting citations in that forum. By attending a media workshop on your campus, you may connect with others developing multimedia programs. At a local conference, you might identify experts in the State on bibliographic instruction who will share program ideas and examples.

Consider yourself in an exploratory mode and look for leads anywhere and everywhere. Talk to people outside your library, outside the discipline, off-campus, at parties, and in the market. Be open to the unexpected. You will probably find related information appearing everywhere—in newspapers, the media, books you've been wanting to read, and spontaneous conversations. Once you open yourself to the possibility, serendipity and synchronicity are likely to occur. Let this stage be fun and stimulating. If you initiated the process with reluctance or dread, enthusiasm may be sparked at this point.

The point of this step, similar to the descriptive exploration stage in the library research process, is to learn enough about the subject and how best to learn more about it in order to develop a strategy.

4. CREATING A PLAN

1. Based on your personal learning style and the parameters of your project, imagine the ideal scenario for you to learn about the subject. Don't limit your creativity to stay within the bounds of possibility or reality.

Imagine the ideal scenario for you to learn.

- What would the environment be like?
- What resources would be available to you?
- How much time would you allow and how would you structure it?
- Would you plan a detailed agenda or let the process evolve spontaneously?
- Would you work in isolation or with others?
- What else is important to you as a learner?

For example: I know I like to immerse myself in a new research project for a long period of time. I prefer a complete break from daily routines and surroundings. I like to take long walks and sit outside in beautiful settings. I like a lot of solitude, but also opportunities to explore ideas with others. I need access to a research library and word processor. I need lots of notecards and colored pens and pencils. Ideally, then, I would take a cabin for at least six months on a mountainside overlooking the ocean but within walking distance of a major research library. I would take the supplies listed above as well as a modem and a fax. I would spend the first week in the library compiling a working bibliography, checking out books, and photocopying articles. Then I would spend some months in passive assimilation: reading whatever appealed to me, interspersed with walks and contemplation, and taking lots of notes that would just go into a pile without being organized. Eventually, I would start talking to people and attending lectures and workshops related to the topic. When I felt the urge to begin actively assimilating, I would begin organizing my notes and rounding out my bibliography. I would make a prioritized list of readings for the mornings and start to write in the afternoons. I would stay at the cabin until I fully developed in writing whatever picture or concept resulted from this process.

Though this obviously describes an idealized situation, the results of this exercise define the parameters within which you can shape your essential framework for a successful professional development effort.

2. Rework your ideal scenario within the constraints of possibility and reality.

OK, so I *can't* spend the next six months in a cabin. But, knowing that I require a break from the routine to center my energy in a new direction, perhaps I *can* adjust my work schedule to free up a few days or a few hours every day for a week or more. At the least, I could take some long walks to clear my head momentarily. Knowing that I need to be "in process" over time, I could claim some hours each week to work on my bibliography, retrieve items, and do some reading by scheduling them on my calendar as I would committee meetings and exercising the commitment to respect those times. I can let the process capture my interest and carry me along. I can structure periods of both passive and active assimilation and both solo and interactive engagement. Of course, if the outcome is time driven, it may be more difficult to accommodate all of my preferences, but at least I can make some choices at the outset. The goal established in the first stage both motivates and determines the parameters of the project.

3. List steps; develop timeline.

Under ideal circumstances, I would let the process develop a life of its own. In reality, it works better to structure the project. Make a list of activities required for the project (include the first three stages outlined here if they are not yet completed) based on your learning style and the project's parameters. For example:

- Developing working bibliography
- Retrieving available items
- Requesting ILL, checked-out items
- Reading and notetaking
- Discussing with colleagues, others

- Attending workshops, conferences
- Learning by doing
- Compiling results
- Responding to and organizing notes
- Applying results

Order the activities as you expect to initiate them. However, don't expect the process to be linear. The bibliography will continue to grow and be refined as the project continues, for example. It is often tempting to prolong the reading, which may cut short subsequent activities; but as additional relevant materials come to your attention, it may be entirely appropriate to make time for them.

Approximate the amount of time required for each activity. Determine the completion date and work backwards from or forwards toward them. Make adjustments in the allotted time periods and plot on a calendar. Although you will probably readjust your timeline, it serves as a reminder of remaining tasks, which can be rescheduled with forethought.

For example: Goal (Need and Outcome): I need to learn to navigate the Internet in order to prepare instructional materials for the fall semester. Personal Learning Style: "Developing a puzzle"—finding "pieces" by reading, discussing, attending workshops, and experiencing periods of passive and active assimilation through which an emerging picture or concept is developed and refined.

Plan (based on ideal learning scenario):

Steps

1. Secure approval (add to annual goals; request release time).
2. Survey the subject or skill to be learned:
    a. Read for background and assimilate passively: "What picture will emerge?"
        1) Look for relevant material in regularly routed items.
        2) Conduct library search and retrieval.
        3) Peruse/organize personal file.
        4) Read and gather more reading material.
        5) Determine components of subject to prioritize for learning.
    b. Talk to colleagues.
    c. Attend campus and local workshops.
3. Learn by doing: experience the Internet.
4. Assimilate actively (including visual depictions).

5. Develop skills, i.e., more focused reading, discussion: "What pieces are missing? How can I more fully develop this picture?" Prioritize components to work with.
6. Begin drafting.
7. Develop instructional materials.
8. Assess/modify plan.
9. Develop continuously (deepen skills, add to/revise materials).

Timeline

Immediately
Immediately and ongoing
3rd week in June
3rd week in June
4th week in June
4th week in June
4th week in June and ongoing
4th week in June and ongoing
End of June–early July
Early–mid-July
Mid-July–early August
August
Late August–early September
Throughout
Use/read about Internet at least once weekly hereafter

4. Secure resources, approval, etc.

Depending on your particular organization, you may have to requisition supplies, hard/software, computer access, a private work space, etc.; or you may have to secure approval for scheduling changes, research leave, workshop or conference attendance, etc.

5. IMPLEMENTING AND MONITORING THE PLAN

Take the first step as soon as possible.
1. Initiate. Your resolve often dissolves in the press of day-to-day responsibilities. Know that it will be difficult to adhere to your timeline and allow yourself the flexibility to make appropriate adjustments.

Keep an ongoing record of what you are learning and how.
2. Compile Results. Consistent with your personal learning style, use notecards, outlining, annotated bibliography, written report (perhaps for publication), audio recording of your thoughts, or visual schema, etc., to keep an ongoing record of

what you are learning and to provide final documentation of your experience. In addition, keep a personal log/diary/journal of your *process* (as you did for the meta-learning exercise) in order to monitor the effectiveness.

3. Assess/Modify. As you progress through the project, use your personal record to evaluate the effectiveness of your plan regularly and make modifications as desired, keeping your goal in mind.

4. Apply the results to accomplish your goal. If your need and outcome are focused on instructional content, for example, at this point you would translate what you learned into curriculum and methodology. Your new conceptual understanding might suggest a metaphor or analogy for hooking your audience, a conceptual framework for organizing instruction, or new content to integrate into library sessions. Develop new instructional objectives and consider a variety of teaching methods to address your students' range of learning styles. Infuse your instructional activities with your new knowledge.

Applications suggested by some of the other examples of goals provided earlier include improving handouts, developing visual or multi-media aids, using the Internet to answer reference questions, training colleagues, producing library publications, implementing new management techniques, enhancing cataloging practice, and selecting a new automation system.

6. INTEGRATING PROFESSIONAL DEVELOPMENT INTO YOUR PROFESSIONAL LIFE

Rework the most effective aspects of your plan as a continuing commitment to professional excellence and personal growth.

Now that you have developed and implemented a project-based professional development plan tailored to your personal learning style, the groundwork will be laid for maintaining education and training as a routine component of your daily professional responsibilities. Take some time to reflect upon and assess this *process*, just as you considered your own learning process as part of the meta-learning exercise. Rework the most effective aspects of your plan as a continuing commitment to professional excellence and personal growth. Reshape steps that proved unsatisfactory and incorporate those aspects that were the most effective for you in order to develop a plan for fulfilling a new need and goal, continuing development in the area you have just been working on, or pursuing general professional awareness or idiosyncratic eclectic inclinations.

The use of meta-learning for professional development promotes both heightened awareness and deliberate action based upon self-knowledge. This approach can then be modeled for others when teaching electronic technology.

RECAP OF STEPS FOR DEVELOPING A PERSONAL PROFESSIONAL DEVELOPMENT PLAN

1. Establish a professional development goal: State the need as precisely as possible, coupled with an outcome and goal. The need becomes your professional development *project* and the goal provides motivation and parameters.
2. Identify your personal learning style.
   (a) Designate, and focus on, a learning situation.
   (b) Record the details of your experience and your observations about it.
   (c) Reflect on and assess yourself as a learner.
   (d) Translate your approach to learning into a "system." Embody your system symbolically as an analogy, metaphor, or conceptual framework.
   (e) Practice and demonstrate your evolving method, modeling it for or teaching it to others.
   (f) Learn more about learning styles in general.
3. Survey the subject or skill to be learned: Consult with others, peruse some literature, use electronic discussion lists, or attend workshops or conferences.
4. Create a plan.
   (a) Imagine the ideal scenario for your learning style and the parameters of your project.
   (b) Rework your ideal scenario within the constraints of possibility and reality.
   (c) Structure the project with a timeline.
   (d) Secure resources, approval, etc.
5. Implement and monitor the plan.
   (a) Take the first step as soon as possible.
   (b) Keep an ongoing record of what you are learning and how.
   (c) Evaluate the effectiveness of your process regularly and modify the plan as needed.
   (d) Apply the results to accomplish your desired outcome.
6. Integrate professional development into your professional

life: Rework the most effective aspects of your process as a continuing commitment to professional excellence and personal growth.

META-LEARNING

Meta-learning is one way to describe the process of articulating, refining, and modeling one's own approach to learning. According to *Webster's Ninth New Collegiate Dictionary* (1986), the prefix "meta" means "1a: occurring later than or in succession to: after . . . b: situated behind or beyond . . . c: later or more highly organized or specialized form of . . . 2: change: transformation 3: more comprehensive: transcending <metapsychology>—used with the name of a discipline designed to . . . deal critically with the original one <metamathematics>." "Meta" preceding a process, then, connotes deliberate, thoughtful awareness and analysis achieved from a position that affords perspective. A growing body of recent scholarship, for example, focuses on meta-analysis or the analysis of the literature on a topic. In learning theory, metacognition or "thinking about thinking" is of interest. For the teaching librarian, meta-learning offers an approach for learning how to learn in order to both keep in stride with the rapid pace of technological development and professional advances and effectively teach evolving resources to users. It is a learning process that can be modeled for students to improve their learning as well.

Meta-learning is a mindful process in which we become aware of, develop, and model our own unique learning style. This is a four-part process.

1. Observe: witness your own process.
2. Reflect/Assess: consider your process.
3. Methodize/Characterize: articulate your process.
4. Expand: vary, add to, or innovate from your process.

Below, we examine how the parts of this process work.

1. Observe: witness your own process.

Designate, and focus on, a learning situation. Choose an occasion when you will have enough time to do this step and the next one. One very appropriate situation is familiarizing yourself with an electronic database or vendor software. You could also consider learning how to use a spreadsheet or computer game, mastering a new kitchen gadget or shop tool, learning a new sport or board game, absorbing a lecture, or acquiring any new skill.

Record the details of your experience and your observations about it. The process begins with awareness. As you engage in the designated activity, record the details of your experience and your observations about it. Ask yourself:

- How do I learn?
- What thoughts are in my head?
- What questions come to mind?
- How do I go about answering them?
- How do I feel?
- What steps do I engage in?
- How do I organize them?
- How do I pose a problem, gather information, form hypotheses, validate data, choose to accept or reject hypotheses?

For example, the Meta-Learning Search Log on p. 18 suggests a structure for using an electronic database as the learning activity.

2. Reflect/Assess: consider your process.

Reflect on and assess yourself as a learner. Immediately following the learning situation, take some time (allow at least 15 minutes) to consider your experience. *Without judging*, ask yourself:

- Do I conduct each step primarily with my intellect, intuition, movement, rhythm, or feelings?
- Do I prefer to engage visually, aurally, spatially, interpersonally, or intrapersonally?
- How consistent or varied are the steps from situation to situation?
- When do actions feel natural or forced/expected?
- What do I prefer or resist?
- What are my strengths and weaknesses as a learner?
- At what points do I feel the most engagement, competence, excitement, fear, dread, dismay, etc.?
- What feels like the best way to engage in this process of observation: thinking about it? recording or journaling it? writing about it? talking about it? drawing it? reenacting it? singing or dancing it? sleeping on it?

In this step, it is important to acknowledge any resistance, struggle, resentment, or feelings of being overwhelmed or scared. Such natural and legitimate responses are an important part of any learning experience and need to be recognized. They often can be managed simply by acknowledging and allowing them. If they persist, it may help to provide voice and relief for such feelings—try talking about them, forming a support group, writing, visualizing, walking, or other forms of exercise.

Try at least two formats for recording or otherwise engaging in your observations.

3. Methodize/Characterize: articulate your process.

Translate your approach to learning into a "system." Embody your system symbolically as an analogy, metaphor, or conceptual framework. The next step may be easier after some time has elapsed. Step away from your learning experience and view it from outside. Translate your approach to learning into a "system": create a multidimensional list of steps, outline, flow chart, or diagram. Then embody your system symbolically as an analogy, metaphor, or conceptual framework.

Metaphor: " . . . how we picture things." (*Harper Handbook to Literature,* 1985, p. 283); " . . . imaginatively identifying one object with another and ascribing to the first object one or more of the qualities of the second or investing the first with emotional or imaginative qualities associated with the second." (*A Handbook to Literature,* 5th ed., 1986, p. 298) A metaphor is implied, whereas a simile is explicit with terms such as "like," "as," or "as if."

Analogy: "A comparison of things similar in a number of ways. An analogy is frequently used to explain the unfamiliar by the familiar, as . . . a camera . . . to the human eye . . . the heart's structure . . . to a pump's. . . . The numerous similarities common to analogy tend to differentiate it from simile and metaphor, which depend on a few points of similarity in things fundamentally dissimilar. Similes and metaphors, however, are sometimes extended into analogies." (*Harper Handbook to Literature,* 1985, p. 31)

Conceptual Framework: " . . . general principles drawn from a field of study and used to organize the content of an instructional presentation. They are the principles which are used to structure classes, courses, and textbooks. Conceptual frameworks may be explicitly discussed as part of a presentation or used implicitly to provide a meaningful sequence for the information covered." (*Conceptual Frameworks for Bibliographic Education: Theory into Practice,* ed. Mary Reichel and Mary Ann Ramey. Littleton, CO: Libraries Unlimited, 1987, p. 3) This is the definitive work on conceptual frameworks in bibliographic instruction. In the first chapter, a reprint of a 1981 JAL article, the editors define the concept and provide brief examples of seven conceptual frameworks. The remaining chapters offer in-depth discussion of 15 conceptual frameworks, such as particular disciplines, systematic literature searching, index structure, and publication sequence.

For example, I used the Meta-Learning Search Log to observe my experience in using an electronic database for the first time. During my period of reflection, I noted that I began by the seat of my pants—simply attempting to conduct my search by transferring known techniques. Then, I fumbled around a bit, learning from successes and failures, and getting some sense of what that database was like and what I didn't know. Finally, I went into the Help screens that provided an organized explanation within which I could position what I understood and fill in what was still unclear, while developing an overall comparative structure in my mind. Now I felt ready to effectively conduct my search.

I realized that, in fact, I am very consistent in such an approach, which I could characterize as developing a puzzle. I like to start a research project by "haphazardly" gathering "pieces," generally quotes and notes and thoughts on index cards. Then I begin to notice that some of the pieces fit together and others are missing. I notice connections and patterns, and I begin to impose some organization. I become interested in the developing bibliographic structure and gathering more information through focused reading. After pieces have accumulated, I usually experience a "click" moment when a larger picture or concept occurs to me, within which the pieces seem to fall into place and fit together, although missing pieces will still be evident. With that big picture, however, I can devise a plan to find those pieces and perhaps to develop the picture more fully. I have used this "developing a puzzle" approach successfully throughout my life, and it is likely that it would be useful for others as well, if modeled or communicated.

4. Expand: vary, add to, or innovate from your process.
Experiment with and improve your approach, modeling it for or teaching it to others. Now that you have observed, described, and named your own learning process, use this awareness to experiment with and improve your approach. Capitalize on your

strengths and build in ways to enhance areas of underdeveloped potential. Then, deliberately or mindfully, practice your approach. This can be accomplished dynamically by demonstrating your evolving method, modeling it for or teaching it to others.

For example, knowing that I will unconsciously enter into the process of "developing a puzzle," I could deliberately set up a learning endeavor to maximize that approach. I could initiate the process by posing the question "What picture or concept will emerge?" I could capitalize on my visual orientation by sketching schema or rough (I'm no artist!) depictions as I go. I could allow time to visualize, perhaps jotting down notes about images that may occur to me spontaneously. I could spread out all my note cards as if they were, in fact, puzzle pieces. Knowing that kinetic learning is my weakness, I could challenge myself to incorporate movement or rhythm in my learning process.

Later, at the Reference Desk or in the classroom, I could talk out loud about how I go about developing a puzzle in a particular instance. I could suggest to a student that she or he look at what is known about a topic or a database as if it were the pieces of a puzzle and ask for consideration of what picture or concept the pieces suggest and what is missing. Some students are likely to be very attracted to this approach, while others will find it pointless; and in the process of modeling or teaching my own approach, I will find it developing and changing dynamically.

META-LEARNING SEARCH LOG

Part I: Observing

Observe how you learn to use a database from a vendor you have never or rarely used. Use the log sheet to record your learning process. Start with your responses to this process:

- What thoughts are going through your head as you start?
- What questions come to mind?
- What feelings?
- What aspects of your surroundings are you aware of?
- What topic are you going to search in the database? Why?
- What preparations for searching do you go through before you actually begin to search and why?
- What are your expectations?

Search the database. Keep close attention to what you do and why and to the database itself and your expectations of it. Examples of things to notice:

- What do you expect from an opening screen?
- Does this database meet that expectation and what effect does that have on how you proceed and on how you feel about the process?
- How involved with your topic do you feel?
- What are you learning about your topic and how to access it?
- How "user friendly" are the commands and functions in this database?
- What do you feel as you go through the search?
- When do you feel comfortable? Frustrated? Anxious? Confident?

The following log sheet is arranged in several broad categories by way of helping you to be mindful of the multiple dimensions of learning. But feel free to redefine the categories or record your learning experience as a simple narrative. The main point is to observe how you learn and to record some of the details of your observations in whatever way works for you.

Search Log:
What I Did and Thought

Why

What Happened

How I Felt

Other

Part II: Reflecting/Assessing

Reflect on and assess yourself as a learner (but only in a non-judgmental way!). Go back and read through the log you just wrote.

How would you characterize the learner revealed in the log? (Draw on other learning experiences you have had as well.)

How does the learner approach learning an unfamiliar database? Systematically? Serendipitously? Anxiously? Confidently?

In going through the search process, does the learner reflected in this log rely largely on intellect? Past experience? Intuition?

Does the learner turn frequently to online aids or prefer to learn through trial and error? Does the learner seek (or want to seek) advice from or interaction with other(s)?

What kinds of expectations does the learner have for this database and what does the learner do (and feel) when these expectations aren't met?

How does the extent of involvement with the subject matter color or shape the learner's experience of the database?

What strengths does this learner seem to have? What weaknesses?

At what points in the search does the learner seem to feel most engaged? Competent? Excited? Fearful? Angry? Why?

In what ways (if any) was the learner's ability to learn affected by this process? By the physical setting within which the activity occurred?

In one or two paragraphs summarize your reflections on yourself as a learner.

REFERENCES

Claxton, Charles S. and Patricia H. Murrell. *Learning Styles: Implications for Improving Educational Practices*. ASHE-ERIC Higher Education Report No. 4. Washington, D.C.: Association for the Study of Higher Education, 1987.

De Bello, Thomas C. "Comparison of Eleven Major Learning Styles Models: Variables, Appropriate Populations, Validity of Instrumentation, and the Research Behind Them." *Reading, Writing, and Learning Disabilities* 6 (July 1990): 203–222.

Fuhrmann, Barbara Schneider and Anthony F. Grasha. "Designing Classroom Experiences Based on Student Styles and Teaching Styles." In *A Practical Handbook for College Teachers*. Boston: Little, Brown, 1983. 101–134.

Keefe, James W. *Learning Style Theory and Practice*. Reston, VA: National Association of Secondary School Principles, 1987.

2 BEING EFFECTIVE IN THE CLASSROOM

Carol M. Withers
New Mexico State University Library

The intent of this chapter is to help instructors reflect upon various aspects of learning, the learning environment, and the student as well as on their own role as trainer/teacher. Some specific techniques and approaches are presented, not as an exhaustive list but as grist for the self-evaluation mill. There may be very little if anything new to the seasoned teacher, but whether you are a veteran or a novice, such review serves as a valuable way to keep teaching fresh and effective.

There are many slick presentation tools from laser pointers to multimedia packages. While these are valid ways to enhance presentations, giving presentations and teaching are not the same thing. You need to keep in sight that the focus of teaching is the subject matter (second only to the students) and communication of that focus is the aim. In this sense, teaching in an electronic classroom is much the same as teaching in a traditional classroom. Instructors with such experience possess valuable transferable skills. Some of us are teachers who are learning the technology to be able to teach it. Some may be knowledgeable about the technology and are learning how to teach. The competent teacher both knows the subject matter and how to teach. In truth, the same investment of time and effort is required to master either.

There are two sections to this chapter: planning lessons and teaching techniques (includes interacting with the students personally and via classroom materials and equipment). Since asking and answering questions are often the primary method of verbal classroom interaction and are frequently considered most challenging to many instructors, a substantial section has been devoted to this.

PLANNING LESSONS AND THEIR EXECUTION, BUT HOPING THEY DON'T DIE

Most often, discussion on classroom preparation focuses on how to write goals and objectives for a lesson plan. This chapter will refrain from that because such literature is abundant and accessible. This should not be taken to mean that it is of little importance. We will, however, discuss the various stages of lesson plans, their value, and some implementation ideas. The lesson plan form at the end of this chapter can be copied and adjusted to your style. It is imperative to know exactly what you want the students to learn, and making a lesson plan helps to clarify that.

OBJECTIVES

The objectives should be clear to the instructor so that they can be made clear to the students from the outset. When a question or circumstance in the classroom looks as though it may take you off track, it is the preconceived lesson plan that will answer the questions:

- What do I need to teach in this period?
- Computer skills?
- Information retrieval?
- Subject matter?
- Problem solving?
- How to use this library?
- How to get through this school year?

If the student's question supports your goal, you can comfortably, and with good conscience, use it rather than your plan as a springboard to dive into your objectives.

Writing out lesson plans helps the instructor prioritize objectives, create a time frame for the class, think through specific techniques, pick out places where handouts and overheads will be of use, and enter the room with all the necessary equipment, overheads, handouts, and items for show and tell—all of which calms the nerves of a novice teacher and generally results in a more organized presentation. Organization does not preclude spontaneity or adaptability to classroom circumstances, but rather allows for worthy transgressions from the plan by solidifying the goals in the instructor's mind.

MOTIVATION

The ideal lesson begins with motivating the learner; for example, tell students what they will get out of the class, even if it is just a faster way to do their homework. Provide a brief overview of what will be covered. Motivating a classroom of students to learn is a balancing act. Think of trying to teach a dozen six-year-olds how to swim. There are the invincible, fearless know-it-alls who are jumping into the deep end; and there are those who are truly afraid. How do you put healthy respect for the water into the plungers, letting them know they don't know it all without squelching their boldness toward learning, while at the same time you are convincing the more timid that the water is fine, fun, and navigable?

In the electronic information classroom, the situation is the same. You must convince the timid they can learn and, in the same sentence, convince the know-it-alls that they don't know it all and it is worth their while to listen. A few comments to the know-it-alls could include:

> Technology changes so fast that nobody can know it all. Even those who use it every day find it challenging to keep up with all the new things in addition to the changes. I took two days off and when I came back there were three new databases to learn.

> The Internet is a living, breathing beast with its own moods and temperaments. It is constantly growing and that growth precipitates change. Parts, sometimes our favorite parts, die and slough off just as with any scaly monster.

And to the timid:

> Similar to Beauty's beast, the Internet is rather nice and has some rather neat stuff that it will share if you ask it correctly.

> For me, it's similar to my car. My knowledge of the internal combustion engine is from the fourth grade. I neither know nor care to know how it works, but it gets me where I'm going. I don't need to know about the nuts and bolts of the Internet. I'm more interested in what the beast has to offer and where it can take me than how it got to be a beast. If I can do it, trust me, you can do it. I'm not mechanically minded. (If, indeed, you are not.)

And to capture those who just do not want to be in class:

Information technology is not the wave of the future. It is here and it is now. Many of our grandparents had to learn to read to survive in their changing world. You have to learn information technology to survive now.

To hold the students' attention throughout class, use examples and demonstrate things of interest to them. As writers and comedians say, know your audience. For example, show grant information to administrators and lyric databases to teens. As learners come and go from these information sources, they will see other things of interest to explore.

PRESENTATION AND GUIDED PRACTICE

Then present the material and/or give a demonstration. Ideas for presentations are in the **Teaching Techniques** part of this chapter. Guided practice follows presentation. This entails the students doing what has been demonstrated or working with the material in some way. In libraries, this would often mean a problem-solving exercise or hands-on opportunity using worksheets or handouts as guides. The instructor circulates. Review what has been taught by emphasizing three, or maybe four, main ideas you want retained. Often this is basically what you promised would be covered. Finally, share the questions or problems raised during the guided practice.

EVALUATION

Let the students know beforehand how their work will be evaluated, if it has an impact on an overall class grade, and whether or not it will be collected. In addition to this, informing the learners in advance if their work will be instructor-graded, self-graded, or graded by peers, reduces anxiety. In many instances of teaching information technology, grading is not an issue. However, this does not mean evaluation can't take place through oral questions or an alert circulating teacher during guided practice. After evaluating what has been learned, re-teach what was exposed as poorly understood. While it is good to present material in a variety of ways, it is not always necessary to create a brand new method to present the material when re-teaching. Often redundancy, re-iteration, or doing it one more time does the trick.

Session evaluation, reflecting on the effectiveness of class time as distinct from the evaluation of students, is important if you wish to continue to grow in your craft. This is doubly important to maintain a comfort level between instructors if a session is team taught. Take time to note what worked and didn't work, to mark an improvement on an overhead or handout, or to write down a new analogy that came to mind.

If you have the opportunity to be observed by peers, set ground rules such as letting them know if you do or do not want them to participate in the class. Be specific in what you want them to observe. For example, ask them:

- Do I explain sequences clearly?
- Do I ask/answer questions well?
- Do I get off the topic at times? Look to see where this happens.
- Do I favor one side of the classroom, or one gender over another?

Focusing observers' attention on one or two of the kinds of things that you want them to observe helps them be constructive and ensures their comments will be on issues you are ready and willing to consider.

Clear lesson plans should exist for each class period, complete with goals and objectives that support the overall week, month, semester plan, or course curriculum. The ideal is certainly not linear. Re-teaching occurs when questions arise. Need for additional worksheets may become apparent midway through. (See the following chapter on hand-out development.) The implementation of these steps vary with size of the group, and the materials and equipment available.

BRINGING THE IDEAL TO THE REAL WORLD

The ideal starts to fade when you have a one-hour session and will never see the learners as a whole class again. Yet valuable teaching can still take place and all the steps in the plan can be implemented, admittedly in an abbreviated format. Flexibility is key. Hands-on experience can be provided in self-guided worksheets. Evaluation can be done through asking questions. And re-teaching can be accomplished through take-home handouts and by telling the students where further help is available, e.g., the reference desk or your phone number.

INFORMATION LITERACY SETTING

There are a few specific points that should be considered when preparing for an information literacy setting. Ask yourself if the students are there to learn a specific task, e.g., get one book or article for this one assignment, discover the plethora of information sources in their field, or to gain the ideas, concepts, and techniques required for them to continue to learn with a certain degree of independence? Be sure the learners are aware of your approach at the outset. If they know you are presenting only a multitude of sources on a topic, and not the intricacies of the technology, the students will not be frustrated at the end of the class. These approaches, as with most things in life, are not mutually exclusive. A mix is frequently what is needed to serve the needs of a specific group. This is where written goals and objectives are extremely important. If the learners need to fulfill a classroom assignment, the instructor needs to decide whether to teach one command (CD) in depth, give an overview of CDs in general, or teach only the CDs that will get the learners through the assignment.

TEACHING TECHNIQUES

Now the plan is made and the class has started. What to do next? You bring your own style and personality to the classroom. Some techniques are universal, such as not standing in front of the overhead-projector light or talking with your nose to the board. Those are not the kinds of things addressed here. Other kinds of techniques need to be adapted to personal style. Keep that in mind throughout this chapter.

INTERACTION WITH STUDENTS

Answering Questions

It is important to recognize questions that are beyond the scope of your goals. It is best if you can relate them to the matter at hand. If there is no way to relate it, the old standby, "Good question, but that won't be covered today; see me after class if you want to pursue this," is always handy. But you must then be willing to pursue it after the session. If you find the question beyond the scope of your expertise, say so. Some believe that to give the impression that the teacher knows it all creates confidence in the learner. However, it is okay not to know it all and it is good for students to see that it is okay not to know it all. Admitting ignorance gives the instructor the opportunity to be a model of life-long learning and to demonstrate the learning process and information-gathering skills. The instructor can offer to get back to the pupil or, in the case of a visit to a school, get back to the pupil's teacher with the information. At such time, the information requested is even more valuable if the process of learning or finding the information is also conveyed. For example, "I found an article on X by using the publicly accessible CD-ROMs at the university library," or "I found an organization in the *Encyclopedia of Organizations* that should be able to help you with your inquiry." This kind of response not only alerts the learner to these kinds of resources, but also places the librarian in a learning partnership with the individual, a more open relationship that the pupil may feel freer to use in the future. It cannot be emphasized enough that this kind of respectful interaction is desirable with people of any age.

Students' questions can turn into the life of the party. The topic of a question can be recalled throughout the session to tie things together, provide examples, and encourage other questions by validating the earlier one. If a question concerns a topic that you will address later, evaluate it to determine if it is best to wait until you reach that point in the session. If so, let the inquirer know you will be answering it later and, at that time, acknowledge both the question and the student. This again validates the question and creates a more interactive feeling in the session. "And this is getting back to the question/point you brought up earlier."

Responses to questions can be a straightforward answer, a question in return, a story, an example, an analogy, a reference to a previously discussed point, or an "I'll get back to you." Straightforward answers are often easiest and take the least amount of time. Questions answered with questions (which can be as simple as "What do you think?") can produce a very interactive session. Instructors using this approach should be prepared to lose some control of the class temporarily while exploring the proposed answers. Guiding the student to a solution often results in a more memorable answer than the one you might have given and is often more fun.

Don't be disappointed in yourself or the students if you are asked a question on something you have just covered. You may have been unclear. The questioner may have dozed (it happens), been trying to digest some other point you had made, or been confused. Repetition, in general, is beneficial. Questions show that they are thinking, not that they are incapable of understanding. When you stand in front of a group, they look at you respectfully as a master of information gathering and evaluation. In return, you should look respectfully at them as intelligent masters of things you may never know and, therefore, capable learners.

Depending on your style, you can accept questions as you go along, at specific times in the session, or at the end. Let the students know at the beginning of the session what is acceptable to you. "Please hold your questions until I ask for them / until the end." If you are willing to take questions as you progress, it may be necessary to stop occasionally and ask for questions just to get the ball rolling. Depending upon the age and culture of the group as well as individual personalities within the group, the waiting time for questions will vary. If you've been working with a group all semester, the time will be shorter than if you will see students only for one hour and then never again. Feel comfortable with silence. Waiting can sprout some good questions that have been germinating while you have been talking.

One cordial approach to a classroom full of raised hands is to acknowledge them all and tell them in what order you will be taking the questions. "Good, lots of questions. You, then you, then I'll get to you." If you find the questions interrupting your train of thought or an idea you wish to complete, acknowledge the question and ask for a few minutes. "I want to get back to you. Let me just finish this idea." For many students, it is an effort to speak in a session and ask a question. This acknowledgment helps those who had to work up the nerve to speak and encourages them not to shy away from asking when it becomes their turn.

At the other extreme, occasionally a pupil will take over the class with her/his questions and anecdotes. If you see the need to stifle, it is important to do so in such a way as not to stifle questions from others. The old, "Let's talk about those things after," response often works, as does the well used refrain, "Thank you, let's hear from someone else." Sometimes students step in because they are uncomfortable with the silence; but if the instructor is comfortable with it, that comfort will often be felt by the students.

Asking Questions

Asking questions is a good way to keep the session interactive. If your more verbal students are taking over by answering all the questions, preface questions with a phrase such as "Someone different now, tell me what...?" In one-time-only sessions, habitually using such a phrase eliminates the need for the instructor to diagnose and cure a take-over artist in the limited time allotted. This prefacing phrase also facilitates broader participation. Again, be comfortable with the ensuing silence and show it in your demeanor.

It is tempting to have a precise answer in your head for the question you put to a class. Rarely, if ever, will you extract the identical answer you have contrived. Be willing to use the terms and partially correct answers elicited from the class to rephrase and clarify the answer. In most situations, it is best to make any answer partially correct or, at least, not totally wrong. For example, when asked, "What's an index, for example, an index at the back of a book?", a student replied with a perfect definition of a glossary. The instructor's response was, "That is a good definition of a glossary which is also found in the back of books. An index is that other thing back there. What is that? What does it do for you?" This response made it clear that the student was not defining an index while acknowledging the knowledge the student possessed. Showing respect for intellect is important in sessions of any age group. Self-esteem is related to ability to learn. Instructors are in the position to boost or squash esteem in front of peers with merely their tone of voice or their choice of words. Go gently.

Traits of the Learners

There are as many kinds of students as there are people in your classroom. Imagine Madonna, a pop star, Picasso, an artist, and Hypatia, a scientist and director of the Alexandrian Library, are sitting in your session to learn all about using the modern library. After you have motivated them and convinced them that they do want to learn, how do you teach them? Books and articles abound dealing with multiple intelligence theory, cognitive strategies, learning styles, perceptual style, thinking skills, etc. The intent of this chapter is not to explore and discuss each of these. Just keep in mind when you prepare for class and when you step into the classroom that Madonna, Picasso, and Hypatia will be sitting there—unrecognized, but they are there.

Be prepared to teach students who relate to the world, process information, and learn in differing ways, for example, through

- Aural senses
- Physical senses
- Visual senses
- Western-style logic and structure

Be prepared to teach in a variety of ways to a variety of learners. It is not a waste of time to verbalize what is on an overhead or handout or to explain a worksheet that includes directions. It is not useless redundancy to explain databases and networks by describing their structure as well as using an analogy, such as the file cabinet as a model. You can offer a choice of either a structured assignment or the freedom to explore with a more fluid worksheet.

Start Where the Learner Is

One of the basic tenets of teaching is to start at the knowledge level of the students, add one piece of information, and, when that is comprehended at a sufficient level, add another piece. This will gradually build the learners' knowledge base without frustrating and discouraging them with information they do not yet have the background to comprehend. It sounds good, but the underlying assumption is that the instructor knows the learners' levels. This is tough in some settings since the learners are often seen only for an hour at the time of instruction. If feasible for the setting, requesting written questions from the students or sending them a questionnaire prior to training may help gear a session to their particular needs. For classes that come to visit the library, the same could be tried, but it is often difficult to get responses. Talking to the class instructor also helps, but may result in inaccurate information such as being told the students know all about X database when they haven't a clue.

One way around this is to start sessions by asking the learners (faculty, staff, or students) questions. Listen to how they respond, the terminology they use, and the completeness of their answers. Are they using jargon correctly? Notice if all the students are keeping up with the one who is giving the answers or if that person is the only one who possesses that knowledge. If only one learner is responding, turn toward the other side of the group and ask a question. Notice the response or lack of response. Ask them for their questions, again noting as above. If they ask for something you are not going to cover, tell them, and let them know where or when they can get the information. "You can sign up for workshop X to learn about that." Truly, this takes less than five minutes since you can usually determine the level accurately enough with only a few interchanges. This exchange also sets up a more interactive relationship for the remainder of the session. It is worth the time.

Be alert to the kinds of questions that arise during a session. Embedded in them may be clues revealing a need to teach material in which the instructor assumed the learners were already conversant. Most of what librarians do is not intuitive (for example, "marking" records to tell a machine that we want to print them later). In addition, most of what is taught in school is related to or based on something previously taught: algebra on number theory, or writing a paragraph on writing a sentence. While times are changing, you still have many learners who have absolutely no pre-knowledge on which to base their library experience. A number of college students still exists who have never touched a keyboard. You must remember that the information you are imparting is falling on many ears for the first time. Paraphrasing Emerson, no one can learn what they do not have the preparation for learning, even if all the information is right in front of them.

Reaching Various Knowledge Levels

In a group consisting of students with varying knowledge levels, "starting from where the student is" still applies. In schoolrooms, teachers deal with this daily. The complaint may arise that some teachers aim at the middle of the group, bore the advanced learners and lose the basic learners. Standard solutions include more one-on-one meetings, review worksheets for the basic student, and tough problem-solving puzzles for the advanced students. While these strategies are also useful in teaching information technology, they may be impractical in settings where the instructor sees the students only once. The instructor could, however, be prepared with different worksheets for a variety of levels. This could create homogenous levels within the larger diverse class but this is not required for learning to occur.

Instructors with groups of heterogeneous knowledge-level learners can facilitate a high degree of learning by ensuring that learners of every level participate. Here are a few ways to do this. If you have a specific assignment, divide it into the number of students in the groups. Tell them verbally and in the written instructions, "There are 12 questions and 3 of you in each group. Rotate so everyone writes the answers for four questions and everyone uses the keyboard. At the top of each section write your name and function for that section. For example: Madonna, keyboarder; Picasso, recorder (writes the answers); Hypatia, advisor (contributes and will have her turn as keyboarder and recorder). Another way to make sure all receive hands-on opportunities is simply to announce when they are to trade places based on time-on-task.

One pitfall to avoid in heterogeneous information-technology sessions is allowing them to mutate into advanced-level homogenous group discussion. No matter how basic a class may be intended, it can deteriorate to involve only the top half of the class and from there turn into a conversation between two or three participants using vocabulary, jargon, and a pace that leaves all others behind. It is the instructor's responsibility to watch for tangents leading away from the objectives and level of the class and to define appropriate jargon as it comes up. It is perfectly acceptable to say, "We won't cover that today, why don't we talk after," or "You're beyond what we will talk about today," or, a personal favorite, "I have no idea, I'll ask and call you tomorrow."

If the instructor has the luxury of determining various levels of a class prior to the session, perhaps more or less homogenous groups could be made and instruction tailored to those levels. This, however, is neither necessary nor even ideal. Heterogeneous groups are often preferred by instructors who find that the higher-level student learns by teaching and the beginner gets more attention, gains more confidence, and may be more likely to ask questions in a small group. Instructors who decide to go this route must have in place ways to ensure that the advanced students don't hog the keyboard, grandstand, or in other ways prohibit the basic learner from participating.

INTERACTION WITH STUDENTS VIA CLASSROOM MATERIALS AND EQUIPMENT

Classroom materials and equipment such as boards, handouts, overheads, and computer screens are there only to help the instructor communicate with the students. It is easy to get stuck up in the front of the room focused on the gadgets, forgetting to notice if the learners are following. Sometimes it's useful to turn your back on the equipment, re-focus on the learners, and ask if they are with you or if they have any questions.

A shared vocabulary is vital to communication. It is easy to forget that the basic terminology you use in your profession is, by definition, jargon and not shared by all our learners. A vocabulary handout may be useful to present at the beginning of the session. If the terms will be used in the session, the instructor has the option of explaining them all at once or as they come up through the session. Going over such a list may be deadly. One way to make it interactive is to list the vocabulary without definitions. Ask the learners to define some terms; the instructor can define the more obscure terms. This allows the students to define things in terms they know rather than having them deal with definitions that may be as confusing as the new vocabulary. It may be best to leave some terms until they can be defined in context later in the session. State that you will be defining terms as you go. Refer back to the vocabulary sheet at the appropriate time so the students can write in definitions.

When you pass out handouts, expect the learners' attention to shift to the handout and away from you. Give them either a moment to look over the handouts or briefly go over them. For example, "We'll be going over the white one first, then the blue which correlates with the demonstration. The others you can read later." This satisfies the natural curiosity you want to encourage and then attention can be shifted back to where you want it. If there are numerous pages, color code or number them for easy referral. Verbally explain worksheets and ask for questions. The best written directions can be misinterpreted.

Overheads, of course, are a good way of showing material visually. A blank sheet of paper under the transparency enables the instructor to see the entire overhead while revealing to the class only what the instructor is currently discussing. This prevents the learners from copying or reading the entire transparency while the instructor is trying to explain the first item. Tell students when a transparency correlates with a handout that has been or will be distributed so they won't write everything down. One way to use transparencies interactively is to produce handouts with only some of the information that is provided in its entirety on the transparency or through explanation of the transparency. Learners can then, in essence, fill in the blanks. Transparencies and computer panels that can be placed on overhead projectors allow the instructor to face the class while keeping an eye on the material placed on the projector.

Overheads as well as white boards also allow the instructor to present material and then wander to the back of the classroom, leaving the students gazing at the transparency or filled white board. The instructor, no longer between the student and the material, can begin to ask questions. The students begin to interact directly with the material. Remember to be comfortable with the inevitable silence. They will either answer your question or ask one of their own.

Demonstrating a specific database is obviously more effective with a computer. Transparencies of computer screens showing the sequence, however, are a welcome relief when the system you want goes down. But let's assume that everything is working as planned. If you are in a hands-on computer classroom and booting is not part of the lesson plan, it is time-saving to have the machines where you want the learners to start. To prevent them from exploring as they sit down to a warm machine, a piece of paper can be taped over the screen obscuring the view. It could read "Welcome to workshop X. Please do not remove this paper until asked to do so," although something with a bit of humor and/or a cartoon would be preferable.

Explain each key stroke as you demonstrate, and if it reflects a choice from a menu, explain why the choice was made. Some audiences will need to be told where on the screen your typing will appear. If you have gone through a complicated set of commands, showing a variety of options along the way, review at the end by encapsulating the minimum sequence needed for students to be successful. "We've looked at several different commands this afternoon. Remember, to get into the database, follow the instructions on the handout. Then type in your terms, press ENTER to look at the results, press F4 to mark the ones you like, then press F2 to download or print. These and the fancier commands we explored are on the blue handout."

Focusing on how best to explain keystrokes, plan lessons, answer and ask questions, create and use handouts effectively, and the myriad of teaching techniques can lead you to forget that your goal is not so much for you to teach as it is to help the students learn. As promised, this chapter falls short of an exhaustive look at teaching. It does, however, cover the basics of classroom survival techniques and attempts to serve as a catalyst for teachers' self evaluation and, by extension, a way to improve your craft. If every time you enter the classroom or have an interaction with a student, you remember that they are capable learners deserving of our time and respect, then you are half way there.

Date:

Class: *Course title if this session is part of a semester-long class*

Lesson plan: *Title for the day or session*

Age/level:

Amount of time:

Goals: *Overall intent of the session/course*

Objectives: *What the learners will be able to do at the end of this session*

Time allotted	Activity	Materials needed
	Motivation: *What you will be doing and why it will be useful for them (agenda can be written on the board or provided in a handout).*	*all the things for show and tell, equipment, over-heads, handouts, worksheets, etc.*
	Presentation of the Material / Demonstration: *An outline for yourself including brief notes to remind yourself of examples, stories, important points.*	*can go in this column right next to the activity it will be used for.*
	Guided Practice: *Teacher circulates and notes questions, problems, and successes to bring to the group's attention during review.*	

	Review: *Discuss issues discovered during the guided practice and concepts that will be evaluated. List them here.*	
	Evaluate: *Discuss the format and grading criteria prior to the evaluation.*	
	Re-teach:	

Follow-up: *Write learners' questions that you need to get back to them about.*

Session Evaluation: *What you want to do differently next time: e.g., less time on motivation / circulate more during guided practice. . . . (Especially important if team taught.)*

The following blank lesson plan may be copied.

Date:

Class:

Lesson plan:

Age/level:

Amount of time:

Goals:

Objectives:

Time allotted	Activity	Materials needed
	Motivation:	
	Presentation of the Material / Demonstration:	
	Guided Practice:	
	Review:	

	Evaluate:	
	Re-teach:	

Follow-up:

Session Evaluation:

3 WRITING FOR INFORMATION LITERACY TRAINING

Donnelyn Curtis
New Mexico State University Library

The complexity of online information systems along with differences in users' learning styles require a variety of instructional aids and approaches. In some instances, written instructions may be the only learning tool available to the user. In other cases, one-on-one or intensive workshop instruction will require supplementary written materials to reinforce the oral lesson or for later reference.

Traditional notetaking is usually not feasible during the demonstration of an online system because the lights may be off. Handouts liberate students from the necessity of writing and allow them to focus their attention on the screen. However, handouts are often an afterthought, thrown together hastily in the face of a workshop. Seen as props, they sometimes don't get the attention they deserve. As stand-alone tools, they might be perceived as something that is needed, but too difficult or time-consuming to produce. A systematic approach to producing written instructions will reduce some of these problems. This chapter will discuss principles and procedures for writing brief handouts for use in an instructional setting or as point-of-use aids for library computer users.

PREWRITING

Going through a process of answering a few questions about the users, purpose, and use for written instructions will result in better handouts, save time, and provide a starting point for what can be seen as a daunting task.

DEFINING THE USERS

Making assumptions and generalizations about an audience is risky but necessary. There may be a wide range of variation, but knowing the general level of sophistication, education, and motivation, as well as the experience and technical skills users can be expected to bring to a new task, will help the writer "customize" the instructions. Knowing the audience for a workshop will influence the presenter's choice of examples and language. Gathering audience information prior to a workshop can be done with questionnaires or an interview with someone from the group; gathering information about other users of written instructions is more of a challenge. The writer must sometimes rely on past experience with similar computer users. Thinking about a specific typical individual whose background is known might suffice.

Thinking about the **subject** background of the users of a system will help the writer make decisions about format and style. Instructions for using a humanities database can include more text and less jargon than you would want to put in instructions for using a scientific database. Instructions for a computer science database might best be presented in a flow chart format.

The probable **computer** background of the users of a system will determine how much and what kind of information should be included. If college users come from the field of education, they might have Apple or Macintosh experience, but they may never have seen an Esc (escape) key. Business majors will be more familiar with the IBM environment. It may seem like a small difference, but taking it into consideration could remove a crucial stumbling block for some users.

The amount and type of computer experience a user brings to the task of learning a new system will influence the amount of detail to be included. Those who are familiar with only Macintosh or Apple computers:

- Will not recognize certain parts of the keyboard (function keys, Ctrl, PgDn, etc.)
- May expect a transfer of learning which does not occur
- Are lost without a mouse

The amount of previous experience that users have with a system will also influence the format and content of a help sheet. To satisfy the different information needs of new, casual, and in-depth users, it may be necessary to produce more than one kind of handout.

New users:

- May have limited experience with retrieval systems in general
- Want to know where to start
- Want to know how the system works
- Want to know what the database includes

Infrequent users:

- Will have a sense of how to begin
- Will usually not remember specific protocols
- Know some of the system's capabilities
- May not be satisfied with a simple search

Frequent users:

- Have learned basic protocols
- May want to learn the most sophisticated features
- May not be using the system efficiently or to its full capacity

DEFINING THE PURPOSE AND PARAMETERS OF THE PUBLICATION

Having a solid sense of a publication's purpose will help make the writing task manageable. If a workshop handout is intended to **reinforce** a presentation and keep the audience oriented, it may need to be only a simple outline of the lecture, or a copy of the overhead transparencies or flip chart diagrams. It is sometimes helpful to have a reference sheet for each participant that provides certain technical information. A glossary of Internet terms can alleviate confusion; a list of field abbreviations for a database can help the audience understand records as they are displayed. The instructor is freed to focus on concepts rather than keystrokes when the students have the system protocols on a piece of paper.

Handouts can **extend** a workshop by providing more information than can be conveyed or absorbed in the time period allotted. Every teacher knows that when a lesson is aimed toward the middle range in any group, some students will be lost and left behind while other students already know what is being covered. One kind of handout can help the left-behind student catch up with the class after the session, while another kind can provide additional challenges to those who are motivated to go beyond what has been covered.

Worksheets can be used before a workshop to give the participants some hands-on familiarity with the basic aspects of a computer system, or they can be used later to encourage the participants to use the system while the knowledge is fresh. "Real" assignments provide the most effective learning experience, but if a group is being exposed to a computer system at a time when members are not required to use it, a worksheet assignment can give the practice that will reinforce the teaching.

Stand-alone handouts can serve a variety of purposes as well. In the absence of a human guide, they can introduce a system, lead the user through a sample search, teach the fine points of using a system, or give the user something to refer to (the cheat sheet).

The purpose of the publication will influence its length and breadth. Most point-of-use guides should not exceed both sides of a single sheet of paper. Tutorials or interactive worksheets, on the other hand, can be several pages in length. There are times, however, when other parameters will play a part. If the instructions are to be posted near the computer, they will need to fit on one side of one page. It is important to know the amount of space you have to work with before beginning to write.

DESIGNING THE DOCUMENT

The information content of the handout is, of course, the central consideration. But the way the information is displayed can make it either usable or inaccessible to readers. Design and style decisions can be made (and modified) before, during, and after you begin writing the content of a handout. The following general principles about organization, layout, typography, and design will apply to almost all kinds of written text. Certain forms of writing require more specialized consideration; this will be outlined following the more general discussion.

ORGANIZATION

Planning what your handout will say and in what order it should be said requires two steps—brainstorming and ordering. Usually brainstorming comes first. After defining the users and their needs and determining the scope of the publication, the writer should jot down ideas about what should be included. If it is a jargon glossary, for example, or a list of important keys and their functions, you would make the list first and organize it later. A long or complex handout might require an outline, which means that the ordering will come first and the content-brainstorming will follow. A task analysis (page 52) should be done before writing computer instructions.

The organization will be determined by the purpose of the handout. A list of terms might be alphabetical, if it is a reference sheet, or in the order in which the concepts described by the terms will be introduced. The decision, in this case, would be based on the anticipated level of the audience; whether you expect the majority of them to be familiar with most of the terminology, and need to refer to the sheet only occasionally, or whether you will be taking most of them to alien terrain and expect them to use the sheet as a guide, reading the terms as you explain them.

LAYOUT

The layout conveys your organization of the information and provides visual cues to help the reader process the information. If the structure of the information is hierarchical, the hierarchy should be immediately apparent. If there are steps to follow, there should be no question that the order is important.

Balance

You will want your readers to read all the information on a page, which means creating a strategic relationship between spaces and text blocks. Too much space in one area, when another area is text-heavy, might cause the eyes to miss what is in the sparse area. Also, an unbalanced page looks wrong. An overall imbalance of a page can make it uninviting. Doing some thumbnail sketches of possible designs can help you avoid pages that are top-heavy or bottom-heavy or too busy in some places or too empty in other places. If your handout contains many short lines, try putting some of the sections in columns.

White Space

"White space" (which will not be white if the handout is printed on colored paper) means the margin areas and the distance between chunks of information. It frames the text and enhances legibility and readability. Research has shown that "chunking" information (presenting it in easily digestible segments) results in more efficient mental processing. If you separate the concepts from each other with white space, you relieve the reader of that mental step. Within a "chunk" that is longer than one line, there should be enough space (leading) to allow the eye to move easily from one line to the next without having to jump. The lines should be together but not crowded together. If a chunk of information is presented as continuous text (paragraphs), in most cases it should have ragged right (unjustified) margins, especially if you are using columns. Research has shown that consistent spacing between letters and words makes text easier to read. Also, when each line looks different, the eye is less likely to lose its place. Ragged right margins are also less formal, more relaxed, and more contemporary than justified margins.

Headings

Headings are the most important cues for orienting readers, allowing them to scan quickly for specific information. Headings should stand apart from the rest of the text through the use of spacing (above and below), location (in the margin or centered), size, font, and/or format (bold, all caps, small caps, italics, etc.). When there is more than one level of headings, you need to make it obvious which headings are subordinate. This can be done through placement, size, or format. It is ineffective to go beyond three levels of headings. If the organization of a text document suggests another level, try putting the information that is subordinate to the third-level paragraphs into a list format, using bullets.

Suggested heading differentiation:

Large, Bold Times Roman	HELVETICA, ALL CAPS	Heading text text text text text
text text text text text	text text text text	text text text text
text text text text text	text text text text	text text text text
		text text text text
Smaller, Bold Times Roman	Helvetica, Upper & Lower	
text text text text text	text text text text	text text text text
text text text text text	text text text text	Subhead text text text text
		text text text text
Text-sized, Bold TR	Smaller Helvetica	
text text text text text	text text text text	text text text text
text text text text text	text text text text	Subhead text text text text
		text text text text
		text text text text

Lists and Bullets

Instructional handouts are not meant to be "read." The information needs to be absorbed or easily referenced, and unnecessary words are obstructions. Paragraphs or even sentences are often not needed. In many handouts, the information structure will resemble an outline without a numbering system.

Parallel subordinate points can be expressed easily in list format as brief phrases. Bullets (originally heavy dots, but now any kind of graphic symbol) can help the reader understand the relationship between listed items: alike but distinct. Avoid using numbers or alphabetical letters to preface listed items unless you want to convey a sequential or prioritized relationship. Numbers should be used to list steps only when the order of their execution is important.

TYPOGRAPHY

Word processing and desktop publishing software offer a dizzying array of choices about typefaces. It is easy to get carried away in experimenting with the variety of what is available, and it is tempting to use as many design features as you can. Experiment, but use restraint! The overall look of your handout should be clean and simple, with cues and highlights only where they are needed. Attractive typography makes the publication inviting and more likely to be used.

Fonts

From the looks of many user publications on display in libraries, some people are still using computers as though they are typewriters with a screen. The Courier font, which is the default typeface on many systems, is also the font found on most typewriters. While there is nothing instrinsically **wrong** with using Courier, it does not convey the image of a cutting-edge library. It has a pedestrian look, dogged by associations with bureaucracy and low-budget production.

In the old days, in-house production of handouts meant using a typewriter, with all its limitations, and anything that needed to look more sophisticated was sent to a printer, where other fonts besides Courier were available. Now, in-house publications can look as if they were professionally printed, so it is a shame not to take advantage of the possibilities. In many cases, upgrading the visual quality of in-house publications is simply a matter of learning how to use another font on your word-processing system. If your equipment is older, your computer's printer may not support all the fonts that are available to you, or you may be required to follow poorly-translated arcane instructions to program your printer to accept another font besides Courier. But it's worth it.

After being freed from the Courier font, many people are confused by the number of font options. Guidelines are in order!

- First, print a "specimen chart" of the fonts available on your system. Some will eliminate themselves immediately from your consideration.
- For chunks of text such as the one you are reading, use a font with serifs. Serif faces offer more differentiation between letters and make sustained reading easier. Sans serif

typefaces, such as Helvetica, provide less visual information.

- If you want to use a sans-serif typeface, they work well for headings, giving a clean look that is well differentiated from the body of the text.
- Avoid flowery or fancy fonts within the body of a handout. If you fall in love with a strong, visually interesting font, use it for the title of your handout.
- Not including your title, don't mix more than two fonts on one page.

Font examples:

- `This is Courier type.`
- This is Times Roman type.
- This is a sans-serif type.
- 𝔗𝔥𝔦𝔰 𝔦𝔰 𝔱𝔬𝔬 𝔣𝔞𝔫𝔠𝔶 𝔣𝔬𝔯 𝔥𝔞𝔫𝔡𝔬𝔲𝔱𝔰.
- *So is this.*
- **This Might be OK for a Title.**
- **You Could Use This for a Title.**
- **OK FOR A TITLE, TOO**
- **ANOTHER KIND OF TITLE FONT**

HIGHLIGHTING GUIDELINES

Visual cues in your handout can draw attention to certain areas and make some parts distinct from other parts. Highlighting techniques can be used to differentiate examples, captions, computer protocols, and anything that should be especially emphasized.

Highlighting in the days of typewriters was limited to the use of underlining and capitalization. Since Courier has been shoved aside by other fonts, you are now encouraged to avoid underlining and capitalizing in favor of some of the other techniques which are made possible with word-processing and desktop publishing software, such as bolding and italicizing. Underlining crowds the text, making it more difficult to read, and words with all uppercase letters are also more difficult to read because words are recognized by their unique shapes, determined by the different sizes of letters. Uppercase letters are all the same height.

Highlighting techniques and formats currently in vogue are italics, bold, color, graphics, and the variation of type size and font. Just as some people get carried away with using exotic fonts when they become available, some novice document designers also get carried away with the use of text highlighting. Again, simplicity should be the overriding principle:

- Less than 10 percent of the text on a page should be highlighted.
- Each type of "cue" (italics, bold, separate font) should denote something different, and the meaning of the cue should be consistent throughout the document.
- The more cues there are, the less they mean; use them sparingly to help the reader process the text.
- All caps should be reserved for major headings and, infrequently, to emphasize individual words in the text. Do not capitalize more than three consecutive words.
- Color should be reserved for occasional emphasis or to show which parts belong together.

ILLUSTRATIONS/GRAPHICS

Desktop publishing systems have greatly increased illustrative and graphic possibilities in document design. Certain graphic tools are built into most word-processing programs as well. "Add-on" clip-art can also extend graphic capabilities, but most packaged clip-art is not as satisfactory as the more artistically inclined might wish. Those with the equipment and the inclination can scan images into documents.

Most systems offer "extended characters" or a font consisting of symbols instead of letters. Some examples of these "dingbat" characters are:

❑ ✳ ➜◆ ❜ ✦ ★ ✚ ➒ ✧ ✩ ◯ ★ ✛ ✝ ☛ ✈

You might want to experiment with the drawing capabilities of your word-processing system. You may be able to draw horizontal, vertical, or sometimes diagonal or free-form lines of various widths, filled or shaded or empty rectangles, ovals, or circles (you can probably make Venn diagrams!).

Designing instructional handouts, once a mundane task, has become a creative outlet. But with graphics and illustrations, restraint is again advised. Once you start bringing visual images into your document, simplicity is difficult to maintain.

- Avoid the temptation to add decorative elements that do not have any other purpose.
- Use illustrations only to help clarify something that is confusing.

- Keep the illustrations near the text that they clarify.
- Use short captions to explain the illustrations, using words found in the text.
- When scanning published images, be aware of copyright restrictions.
- Use graphics to lead the eye where you want it to go.
- Avoid frames around the entire page. Because most photocopiers can't keep pages accurately centered when making multiple copies, the frame will look crooked.
- Be careful with boxes or heavy horizontal lines within a document. They can create a visual barrier.
- Keep shaded (gray) areas fairly light and test to make sure they will photocopy evenly.

You may want to develop or adapt a library logo for use on all of your in-house publications. A well-designed masthead can give your handouts a distinctive identity that projects an image you want to project. You can store an electronic "template" to use for any kind of library publications.

SPECIALIZED FORMATS

OVERHEAD TRANSPARENCIES

It has often been said that "people remember about 10 percent of what they hear and about 20 percent of what they see. But they remember as much as 65 percent of what they hear and see together." Overhead transparencies are therefore valuable instructional aids. Most of the above principles of document design, text formatting, and organization will apply to overhead transparencies, but there are some special considerations in designing something that will be projected to enhance a workshop or class presentation.

- Use only one idea or concept per transparency.
- Put a prominent heading on each transparency to keep the audience oriented.
- Keep the layout and design simple.
- Use graphs rather than tables to display numerical information.
- Avoid vertical lettering—it hinders readability.
- Use bold type.

- Avoid tall, thin, ornate, or flowery fonts.
- Use color sparingly for emphasis.
- Use at least 24-point type (or letter size no smaller than 1/4").
- Check visibility by looking at the transparency from a distance which is six times the width of the page, i.e., from four feet away, if the transparency is eight inches wide.
- Number the transparencies and mark your notes accordingly.

FLIP CHARTS

Flip charts are another visual aid that will reinforce your oral instruction. They require no electrical outlets or special equipment. Carefully designed and executed flip chart pages or partial pages can be interspersed with blank pages and sections of pages on which you can write or draw spontaneously as you speak, bringing some action or interaction to your presentation. Pre-drawn pages allow you to face your audience.

Here are some general guidelines for flip chart design:

- Use no more than 35–40 words on each page.
- Use a heading on each page.
- Use a margin of at least 3–4 inches.
- Leave blank pages where you will want to write or draw during the presentation.
- Leave blank pages between composed pages to prevent the audience from directing its attention to the chart prematurely.
- Use bullets to highlight certain points or to distinguish between different items.
- Keep the bullet size about half the size of the letters.
- Indent subordinate items and distinguish them from the major point with a different bullet or color.
- Number the charts and mark your notes accordingly.

Color is particularly effective on flip charts, but follow these guidelines:

- Use color to draw attention to the center of interest on a page.
- Use color for headings.
- Black, blue, and green offer the greatest visibility.
- Avoid purple, brown, pink, and yellow.
- Use red sparingly; it is best for accents only (bullets, arrows, etc.).

- In most cases, stick with two colors; three can be used if well planned but too much color can cause confusion.

COMPUTER INSTRUCTIONS

Defining the Computer's Tasks

If the purpose of your handout is to provide instructions for using a computer system, you will need to conduct a task analysis—the first step in shaping the information content. Focus on the learner's goals in using the system rather than on the features of the system or basic concepts. Analyzing the steps required to accomplish each task in the process will provide a user-oriented organization for the instructions. User information requirements are generated from the task lists.

In using an online information retrieval system, the tasks might be to

- Plan the search.
- Enter the search terms.
- Evaluate the results.
- Modify the search.
- Capture the results.

There is a procedure for each of the tasks and each chronological step can be expressed as a "task statement." Together these sequential statements will comprise the heart of the instructions. To formulate a task statement:

- Begin each task statement with an action verb.
- Describe the subject of the activity in the second word of the task statement.
- Describe how the task is completed.
- Relate the purpose of the task.

A typical instruction statement will answer the following questions:

What is done? (action verb)	To what is it done? (object)	How is it done? (tools)	What is accomplished? (effect of purpose)

Examples:

Select **Open** in the File menu. The Open dialog box will appear.

Click the right-arrow button once. You should see the next card in the stack.

Design and Format Considerations

Computer instructions require some special attention to the way information is communicated. Even if you are providing instructions for a computer system that is user-friendly, you will need to establish some conventions and use them consistently. Pay particular attention to the way you indicate keystrokes:

- Using another font can be effective.
  - `Courier resembles the typeface on a computer screen.`
  - **Helvetica bold** stands out in the midst of Times Roman text.
- If you use **bold** to indicate keystrokes, be sure not to use it for any other purpose, i.e., emphasis.
- Do not use quotation marks around the words the user is to type. A few users will take you literally and actually type them.
- If you feel you must indicate keystrokes in a more noticeable way than typographic cues will allow, the unelegant **< keystroke >** has become somewhat of a recognized standard. There have been no reports of confused users typing the < > symbols.
- When referring to a key on the keyboard, use the name printed on the key: Esc, Ctrl, F2 *[option]*, etc.

Sometimes it is easier to show a picture of the computer screen than to describe what is on it. Because screen images will take up space on a page, they should be chosen carefully for inclusion. Some software has a feature that allows you to import "screen dumps." However, in some cases, it will be better to use other software features to simulate the screen on your handout. If a screen is packed full of information, and you reduce its size and aren't able to use color, it may be too confusing for the user. It would be better to draw a square (with rounded corners, maybe) that contains the **important** information on the screen that you are trying to highlight. It needs to resemble the actual screen only in basic ways.

The use of examples in computer instructions can help the "active learner" interact with your instructions through emulation. However, they do take up space, especially when surrounded by white space, as they should be. Use them when they will help explain a confusing step; skip them if the step is simple.

User Testing

Computer instructions should not be considered complete until after at least one typical new user has tested them. It is easy for you, the writer, to skip an important step when you are familiar with a system. Users should be observed and interviewed to uncover areas of potential confusion as well as omissions. Be willing to start over from the beginning if several users have trouble using your instructions.

WORKSHEETS/TUTORIALS

Interactive worksheets ask questions that the students will answer in writing. Similar to computer instructions, they take a great deal of advance thought about the user's perspective, and they will benefit from user testing during and after the writing process. A successful worksheet will lead the user through a step-by-step, hands-on process of getting to know a computer system or a research process. It can help students work through a process that is difficult to describe verbally. No one REALLY knows how to use a computer system until they use it. A piece of paper is no substitute for a human teacher, however, and a worksheet will be much more useful if accompanied by some oral explanations.

- The objectives for the worksheet should be clearly understood by the user as well as the teacher. The title may be enough to tell the student the scope of the worksheet; if it does not, then a sentence or two at the beginning might be in order.
- A worksheet should not attempt to cover too much ground. If a basic task has many steps or variations, then one task per worksheet would be enough.
- The students will need to know if the worksheet will be graded and, if so, how much it is worth. You need to make it clear whether or not collaboration is encouraged or allowed.
- The interactivity of a worksheet is dependent on lean text. It is not for reading, it is for doing. The written explanation should be minimal—a successful worksheet will lead users to their own conclusions and understanding.
- Questions should be carefully crafted to engage different levels of thinking and to require some analytical effort.

- Yes/no questions should be avoided.
- Even if a worksheet takes the learner through several progressive steps, the questions should be independent of each other if possible. You don't want anyone to get irretrievably snarled up by not understanding one of the questions.
- Unlike any other kind of handout, worksheets yield feedback on how well they are constructed. If many students have problems with a certain section, you know that you will need to work on it. Keep revising!

SYNTAX TIPS

All of these instructional handouts and visual aids have something in common—economy of words. When someone is learning a new task, particularly if computers are involved, it is not appropriate to spend too much time reading. You are not creating a work of literature, and the task, not your writing, should be the focus. Your writing does not need to be "interesting," it needs to be invisible. Pay special attention to the words you use, and follow a few guidelines to make it easier on your users:

- Use parallel phrase and sentence constructions, particularly in lists.
- Use the active voice (subject, verb, object).
- Use simple language ("start," not "initiate"; "use," not "utilize").
- Avoid nouns created from verbs; use active verbs ("sign the check" not "put your signature on the check").
- Avoid colloquialisms and slang. Some of your readers may not be native speakers.
- Use the second person pronoun "you." Acknowledge that you are guiding your readers through a learning process.
- Don't be too stiff or too casual.

WRAPPING IT UP

A handout that will be used for more than one occasion or will be available on a continuing basis is never "finished." Computer systems and users change; you change and learn. In-house publications can be easily modified in response to any of these changes, using desktop publishing or word-processing software. The typesetting days, when it was as cheap to make 2,000 copies as 200 copies, are gone.

However, there are stages in the development of a handout when it is temporarily complete. Be sure to have someone other than yourself proofread it before you declare it done, and print a master copy using the best equipment you have available. If you have a rack with several handouts, or if you will be providing multiple handouts to workshop participants, photocopy them on different pastel colors of paper. Good contrast between the paper and the print enhances legibility; black print on off-white paper has been shown to be the easiest to read. Pastel paper doesn't have to be hospital green and pale yellow. Lilac, peach, ivory, and blue-gray are some contemporary light colors.

REFERENCES

Allen, Susan M. "Designing Library Handouts: Principles and Procedures," *Research Strategies* 11 n.1 (Winter 1993): pp. 14–23.

Balan, Phyllis. "Improving Instructional Print Materials Through Text Design," *Performance and Instruction* 28 n.7 (August 1989): pp. 13–18.

Felker, Daniel B., Frances Pickering, Veda R. Charrow, V. Melissa Holland, and Janice C. Redish. *Guidelines for Document Designers*. Washington, D.C.: American Institutes for Research, 1981.

National Audio-Visual Supply. *How To Prepare Effective Overhead Projector Presentations: One Picture Is Worth a Thousand Words*. 1992. ERIC Document #ED353967.

National Audio-Visual Supply. *How To Prepare Effective Flip Charts*. 1992. ERIC Document #ED353966.

4 TEACHING THE STANDARD FEATURES OF ELECTRONIC DATABASES

Donald A. Barclay
New Mexico State University Library

When you consider the mind-numbing assortment of electronic databases available via OPACs, CD-ROMs, the Internet, and commercial online services, your first reaction may be to say, "There are no standards!" While it is true that the world of electronic information is far from standardized, some features appear in enough databases to be held up as standards or at least as features an electronic searcher might expect to see in more than one database. In addition, there are a number of standard search strategies that can be applied across a range of electronic databases.

The advantage of teaching about standard features and standard search strategies is that this approach can help students get past the idea that each new electronic database they encounter is an Everest to be climbed from the bottom up. Once students learn that electronic databases are more alike than they are different—that much of what is learned about using Database A can be transferred to Database B—they are on the road to becoming life-long learners who can adapt to changing technology on their own.

It can be helpful to draw an analogy between learning electronic databases and learning word-processing packages.

Learning to use electronic databases is similar to learning word processing. Let's say the first word-processing package you ever used was something called LetterPrimitive. Chances are you invested a lot of effort in learning the use of LetterPrimitive, and you probably experienced a lot of frustration, too. However, if a few years later you switched from LetterPrimitive to CaveWord, you probably found it much easier to learn the new word-processing package. That's because many of the basic word-processing skills you learned on LetterPrimitive transferred to CaveWord. The same is true of electronic databases. Once you learn to use one electronic database, you can apply many of the principles you use with it to each new electronic database you encounter.

What follows is a listing of electronic database features and searching techniques that can be called "standard." Of course not all electronic databases support all the standards listed below, nor would you want to teach every standard listed in this chapter—at least not all at once. As you teach, it is up to you to remind your students that a standard feature may be found on *many* or *some* or *a few* databases, but not on all. Students will learn more if, instead of just describing standards, you demonstrate them on actual electronic databases. And they will learn even more if they are allowed to practice using standard features and search strategies as they go. There is no substitute for practice and actual experience.

In the paragraphs that follow, most features and techniques are not described in full detail. The reason for this is that this chapter is intended to serve as a memory and organizational aid for teachers and trainers who already understand the concepts of electronic searching. Therefore, it wouldn't be a good idea simply to hand this chapter directly to students or read it aloud to them. Direct involvement by a teacher is necessary when dealing with the following information.

JARGON

As you teach standard features and search strategies, you must define the jargon of electronic information for your students. Words like *hits, keywords, databases, download, fields, records,* and *Boolean* come to mind as examples of jargon, but there are many more words that fall into this category. No matter how familiar information jargon may feel to you, do not assume that your students know even one word of it.

THINGS EVERYONE SHOULD KNOW ABOUT ELECTRONIC DATABASES

STRUCTURE OF ELECTRONIC DATABASES

Databases often consist of **records**—whole units of information such as citations, citations with abstracts, or full-text documents. Records are usually divided into **fields**—smaller units of information such as author name, journal title, date of publication, and so on.

LIMITATIONS OF ELECTRONIC DATABASES

No electronic database contains everything. Considerations such as privacy, secrecy, the commercial value of information, and the cost of converting print information to electronic form make it unlikely that there will ever be "The Computer" with all the information in the world loaded on it. Other limitations of electronic databases include:

Subject(s)	Some databases cover a specific subject; others are more general.
Publications/ Information sets	Full-text and bibliographic databases are limited by the finite set of journals, books, conference proceedings, etc. that they index or reproduce. Directory databases are limited by the finite set of phone numbers, persons, businesses, associations, etc. that they include.
Dates	Databases are limited by the date of the information included. For example, a business database may cover only the most recent five years of business information.
Updates	A database may be updated daily, monthly, quarterly, etc.
Timeliness	Even if a database is updated daily, the newest information it contains could be months or years behind what has come into existence.
Self-imposed limitations	The producers of a full-text or bibliographic electronic database may choose not to index or reproduce certain types of information—short articles, editorials, book reviews, cartoons, advertisements, etc.—that appear in publications the database otherwise covers. Database producers may choose not to index or reproduce anything at all from a particular publication because the publication is considered ephemeral, not sufficiently scholarly, too specialized, etc. Language of publication and place of publication can also be factors in whether a database covers a particular publication. Directory databases impose similar limits. For example, an electronic directory of businesses may exclude businesses with fewer than 20 employees or all businesses located outside of North America.
Errors	Electronic databases are limited by errors such as incorrect information, overlooked information,

and various technical errors that may make some information in the database unretrievable. Just because a database is electronic does not mean it is perfect.

ACCESS TO ELECTRONIC DATABASES

Some databases are open to all (public access); other databases are restricted to certain users (for example, the students and faculty of one university). Restricted databases usually require a password before you can access them. You may be able to access some databases from remote locations (via modem, for example); to access others, you may need to go to a specific location (a library or office). Sometimes you may be able to access the same database remotely as well as from a library or other specific location. There may be a number of steps involved in accessing a remote database, and these steps may not be the same in all locations.

When you access a remote database you may not be able to do everything you can do when you access that same database through a more direct connection.

> Example: If you use a modem to access a CD-ROM mounted on a LAN, you may not be able to download or print as easily as you can when you use the same CD-ROM at the site where the LAN is housed.

A database that is public in one form or place may not be public in another form or place.

> Example: A library may offer the MLA database on a CD-ROM workstation that anyone can use free of charge. However, if you use MLA via DIALOG, you may have to pay a fee.

The same electronic database can appear in a variety of forms.

> Example: The ERIC database is available on SilverPlatter CD-ROM, DIALOG, and the Internet.

Different databases can appear in the same form.

> Example: There are many different databases on SilverPlatter CD-ROMs.

Databases that charge for use may do so by charging for connect time, charging a flat rate, charging per search, charging for the number of results printed/downloaded, or some combination of the above. It is virtually impossible to stumble into a commercial database and end up being billed for a service you thought was free. Some electronic databases may be accessed by a large number of users at once; others may be accessed by only a limited number of users at one time. It is possible that you may be denied use of a database because it is serving the maximum number of users at the time you try to use it.

STANDARD FEATURES OF ELECTRONIC DATABASES

HELP SCREENS AND GUIDES

Most electronic databases have help screens that give you important information about searching the database and about what information is included in the database. Often typing **help** or **?**, or pressing the **F-1** key, will bring up help screens. There may be printed guides available to help you use an electronic database. Sometimes these guides are commercially published; sometimes they are published by libraries or other local entities.

CORRECTION KEYS

With very few exceptions, electronic databases allow you to correct typing mistakes and to revise search terms as you type them. Ways of correcting include:

- Backspace key
- Delete key
- Highlight and delete
- Typeover

When using the Internet or connecting via modem, the usual correction keys may not work. If this happens, you can try:

- ^backspace
- ^h
- ^w

(The symbol ^ is commonly used to represent the control (Ctrl) key on the computer keyboard. When a command includes the control key and another key, you must press both keys at once.)

CASE

An electronic database can be case sensitive or case insensitive. On a case-sensitive database, capitalization matters; on a case insensitive database, capitalization doesn't matter.

FUNCTION KEYS

On many databases, commands can be executed by pressing function keys (sometimes called **F** keys). Help screens usually tell you what commands can be executed with function keys. On some databases you may execute identical commands with either function keys or regular keys, depending on which you prefer. Again, help screens usually supply information on this. When accessing databases via modem or Internet connections, function keys may not work.

NEW SEARCHES

Most electronic databases allow you to compose a new search without logging out of the database and starting all over again. They may do this by allowing you simply to type in a new search at any time and/or by allowing you to return to a search screen where the results of your previous searches are displayed and a prompt allows you to type in a new search.

SAVING KEY STROKES

Some electronic databases allow you to avoid retyping the same phrases over and over as you search. Common ways of doing this include:

Grouping search results by line number so that you can reuse search terms by typing line numbers instead of retyping terms.

Saving search statements to a hard drive or a disk so that you can redo the same search at any time in the future.

Saving a search so that it can be transferred from one database to another. This is most often seen on CD-ROM databases where different years of the same database are stored on separate disks.

STANDARD ELECTRONIC SEARCHING TECHNIQUES

When you search an electronic database for information on a topic, you must balance precision with recall. When a search has a high level of precision, there is a danger that relevant information will not be retrieved. When a search has a high level of recall, there is a danger that irrelevant information (false drops) will be retrieved.

FREE-TEXT SEARCHING

Almost all electronic databases allow free-text searching. When you do a free-text search, it is helpful to understand exactly what parts of the database are being searched, i.e., all fields or only selected fields? The full text of every record or only the abstracts?

Most electronic databases have a list of **stopwords**—words that cannot be searched as free-text terms. *The, of, by, in,* and *be* are examples of common stopwords.

Many electronic databases allow you to access an electronic **index** that lists all the searchable free-text words and phrases contained in the database. Often you can select and search words or phrases from an electronic index without retyping them.

Advantages of Free-Text Searching

A free-text search is not limited by your knowledge of the fixed vocabulary used by the database. A free-text search is not limited by the shortcomings of fixed vocabularies, i.e., misassigned fixed-vocabulary terms, archaic fixed-vocabulary terms, lack of fixed-vocabulary terms to describe a specific topic, etc.

Disadvantages of Free-Text Searching

Free-text searching may result in more false drops than fixed-vocabulary searching, and depends on your ability to identify appropriate keywords and their synonyms.

FIXED-VOCABULARY SEARCHES

Some electronic databases have fixed-vocabulary terms attached to each record. Such databases can be searched using fixed-vocabulary terms. Fixed-vocabulary terms often vary from database to database. However, most college and university online library catalogs use the *Library of Congress Subject Headings* for their fixed vocabularies. Depending on the database, fixed-vocabulary terms might be called **subject headings, descriptors, topical terms,** etc.

Thesauri

Most electronic databases with fixed vocabularies have electronic thesauri through which their fixed vocabularies may be accessed. Such databases may also have printed thesauri. Many electronic thesauri allow you to select and search fixed-vocabulary terms without retyping them. Both print and electronic thesauri provide cross references that help you identify the best fixed-vocabulary terms for your topic.

Advantages of Fixed-Vocabulary Searching

Ideally, searching by the appropriate fixed-vocabulary term(s) retrieves all relevant information on your topic without retrieving any false drops. Search barriers, such as language differences, non-descriptive titles, and variant spellings, i.e., labor/labour, Beijing/Peking, are reduced or eliminated by searching fixed vocabularies.

Disadvantages of Fixed-Vocabulary Searching

Lack of familiarity with a database's fixed vocabulary may be a barrier to searching. The shortcomings of fixed vocabularies, i.e., misassigned fixed-vocabulary terms, archaic fixed-vocabulary terms, lack of fixed-vocabulary terms to describe a specific topic, and so on, may result in failure to retrieve relevant information.

COMBINED FREE-TEXT/FIXED-VOCABULARY SEARCHES

Many electronic databases allow searchers to combine fixed-vocabulary searching with free-text searching.

> Example: In a single search you might combine the fixed-vocabulary term "cookery-American" with the free-text word "health" to locate information on cooking healthy American-style food.

BOOLEAN LOGIC

Most databases allow searching with the three Boolean operators—**and, or,** and **not.** You must understand the use of these operators, especially **and,** if you are going to search successfully. Venn diagrams are one way to teach the concept of Boolean logic; algebraic logic is another. A third way is through analogy. See the following boxed text.

The Analogy of the Boolean Cafe

Boolean Cafe logic is the opposite of normal cafe logic. In a normal cafe "soup and salad" means you get more—soup as well as salad. But in the Boolean Cafe, where Boolean logic rules, "soup and salad" means you get less. In fact, in the Boolean Cafe you would get only something that was both soup and salad at the same time—clam chowder salad or Caesar salad soup. Similarly, in a normal cafe "soup or salad" means you get less—either soup or salad, but not both. But in the Boolean Cafe "soup or salad" means you get every soup and every salad in the place. Finally, there is *not*, which is the same in both cafes. "Soup not salad" means the same thing in the Boolean Cafe that it means in a regular cafe—you get soup but no salad.

(This analogy can have more impact if you use bowls and plates to illustrate it.)

Searchers should be aware that some electronic databases supply a default operator (usually **and**) if no Boolean operator is specified in a search.

BROADENING SEARCHES

Most electronic databases allow you to broaden a search in order to improve recall. There are two principal ways to broaden a search: Boolean **or** and **truncation**.

Boolean or

The Boolean **or** is generally used to combine synonyms. Boolean **or** searches usually become part of a Boolean **and** search later on.

Truncation

Truncation symbols vary from database to database, but some common truncation symbols are *, !, ?, and $. Where you place a truncation symbol is important.

Root truncation	You place a symbol at the end of a root word, telling the database you want all words that begin with that root.
Internal truncation	You replace a single letter within a word with a truncation symbol. For example **wom*n** finds **woman** or **women** (but not *wymyn*).

Some databases automatically search all variant forms of every keyword, making truncation unnecessary.

NARROWING SEARCHES

Most electronic databases allow you to narrow a search in order to increase precision. There are three principle ways to narrow a search: Boolean **and**, Boolean **not**, and **proximity operators**.

Boolean and

The Boolean **and** is used to combine two or more search terms in order to increase precision. The Boolean **and** can also be used to combine separate groups of synonyms that have been created using the Boolean **or**.

Boolean not

The Boolean **not** is used to increase precision by eliminating records containing specific keywords or fixed-vocabulary terms. Even more than with the Boolean **and**, there is a danger that use of the Boolean **not** will eliminate relevant records from a search.

> Example: If you are looking for information on W. S. Gilbert and you give the command **Gilbert not Sullivan**, you will eliminate many records containing useful information about Gilbert because those records also happened to contain information about Sullivan.

Proximity Operators

Some electronic databases allow you to use proximity operators to increase precision. Proximity operators are used to retrieve those records in which your search terms appear within a specific number of words from each other, appear in the same sentence, or appear in the same paragraph. Some proximity operators can also specify that the search terms appear in a certain order, i.e., **dog** within one word of **star**, but only if **dog** appears before **star**.

Limiting

Limiting is similar to narrowing in that it can increase precision. Many electronic databases allow you to limit your searches by specific elements in the records. Some of the more common limits include:

Date of publication	Before a certain date, after a date, between a range of dates, or on a specific date.
Language	Either limit your results to a certain language or

	languages, or exclude a certain language or languages from your results.
Publication type	Limit your results to only journal articles, for example. Or perhaps exclude all book reviews from your results.
Location	A union catalog may allow you to limit a search to a particular library or set of libraries whose holdings are included in the catalog.

Some limiting features are unique to a particular database or small group of databases.

Example: The PsycLIT database allows you to limit by a psychological study's population type (human or animal).

Help screens and printed guides can give you information about what limiting features a particular database supports.

Another way of limiting is to limit a search to a specific field such as **author, title, subject heading,** or **abstract.**

Example: When searching a full-text database of court cases, you might limit your search to retrieve cases only where the keyword *Miranda* appears in the title.

TRYING AGAIN

One characteristic of expert electronic searchers is that they keep trying. Experts know that failure to find information on the first try, or on the first few tries, doesn't mean there is no information on their topic. Expert electronic searchers:

Immediately retype a search if it doesn't work the first time. A word may have been misspelled or the computer may not have been "awake" to receive the search the first time it was typed.

Try their search in several databases.

Try different search strategies—different keywords, different fixed-vocabulary terms, different combinations of Boolean operators, etc.

Consult with other experts—librarians, other searchers, subject specialists, etc.

STARTING AN ELECTRONIC SEARCH

CHOOSING A DATABASE OR DATABASES

You must decide which database or databases will best fill your information needs. The database(s) you choose will directly influence the amount of relevant information you retrieve. Choosing the "wrong" database is a common mistake of novice searchers. Sometimes the name of a database will tell you if it will fill your need; sometimes help screens or printed material will give you this information. Your choice of database may be influenced by what databases are available in your area or are available to you free of charge. Asking a librarian or other information expert is a good way to find out what databases will best fill your information need.

DEVELOPING A WELL THOUGHT-OUT QUESTION

Because this is perhaps the most important and intellectually demanding part of conducting any search, it is one that novice searchers often ignore, choosing instead to focus on the mechanics of manipulating the database in front of them. Simply writing down the question you are tying to answer is one of the best ways to develop a good question.

DEVISING A SEARCH STRATEGY BEFORE STARTING YOUR SEARCH

Often a search strategy begins with identifying the best keywords to search. You can do this by consulting a publication (reference source, textbook, article, etc.) on your topic or by asking someone familiar with your topic to suggest keywords. If the electronic database you are using has a fixed vocabulary, examine that fixed vocabulary for terms to search. After you have identified keywords or fixed-vocabulary terms, you should try to identify synonyms for those keywords or terms by: consulting a thesaurus; brainstorming; or talking with someone familiar with your topic.

One common, sophisticated search strategy works as follows:

1. Identify terms that describe the two or more main concepts you wish to **and** together.
2. Identify likely synonyms for each term and group these sets of synonyms together using the Boolean **or**.
3. Combine the **ored** sets of synonyms using the Boolean **and**.

The following boxed text demonstrates how to formulate such a search prior to searching. (Note that only plural forms of search terms are shown. In an actual search, singular forms would also be included.)

#1	#2		#3
Term	_students_	_databases_	_skills_
_or_	_or_	_or_	
Synonym	_learners_	_indexes_	_abilities_
_or_	and	and	
Synonym	_trainees_	_CD-ROMs_	_successes_
_or_	_or_	_or_	
Synonym	_pupils_	_online databases_	
_or_	_or_	_or_	
Synonym		_OPACs_	

(Terms and synonyms may be either keywords or fixed-vocabulary terms.)

A few advanced electronic databases employ artificial intelligence so that you don't have to formulate a search strategy to achieve precision and recall. Common names for such advanced systems include **natural language searching, expert systems,** and **intelligent agents.**

VIEWING SEARCH RESULTS

Once you have conducted a search and retrieved records, you must view those records. While knowing how to search is often stressed when learning to use electronic databases, knowing how to look at the results your search retrieved is just as important.

USING WHAT YOU SEE ON SCREEN TO REVISE YOUR SEARCH

Most expert electronic searchers are good at using what they see on screen to revise and improve their searches. Two of the main on-screen clues they take advantage of are **number of hits** and the **keywords** and **fixed-vocabulary terms** that appear in the records they retrieve.

Number of Hits

Most electronic databases allow you to look at the number of hits a search retrieved before you look at the actual records. Retrieving **a very large number of hits** tells you that your search needs to be narrowed unless you are truly looking for complete recall and are willing to invest the time necessary to painstakingly examine a large number of records. Retrieving **zero hits** or **very few hits** usually tells you that you should broaden your search, try other search terms, or try a different database. However, if your topic is very specialized or you need only a few sources, retrieving **very few hits** may be fine.

Free-Text and Fixed-Vocabulary Terms

If you do a search and pull up some particularly on-target records, look at the keywords and fixed-vocabulary terms that appear in these records. You can then search these keywords and/or fixed-vocabulary terms to retrieve similarly on-target records.

CHANGING WHAT YOU SEE ON THE SCREEN

Many electronic databases offer:

A way to move from a display of your search strategy and number of hits to your results and back again.

A way to specify what is displayed on screen. For example, there may be a way to look at only the titles of records, or citations without abstracts, or all the available information for each record.

A way, in full-text databases, to move from looking at full-text records to looking at only citations and back again.

A way to move from record to record without having to return to a search screen or other intermediate screen.

A way to jump to a particular record without having to move through every other record your search retrieved. Most electronic databases number each record in a set of results so that you can tell where you are as you move through the records.

A way to specify the order of the records displayed. For example, you may be able to have the records you retrieve displayed in order from most recent to oldest, or in alphabetical order by author.

INTERPRETING WHAT YOU SEE ON THE SCREEN

Screens can be difficult to interpret for a number of reasons. The monitor you are looking at may be of poor quality or incapable of showing every on-screen detail that another monitor might show, e.g., you may be looking at a color display on a black-and-white monitor. Screens can be cluttered with information, some of which is not important to you. The ability to interpret screens comes with experience, but there are some tricks that can help you.

Field Labels

In many electronic databases the fields of each record are labeled to help you understand what you are seeing. For example, the label **author** tells you that this field contains information about the author, while the label **journal** tells you that this field contains the name of the journal where the cited article was published. Field labels are often abbreviated in electronic databases, but you may be able to decode these abbreviations by reading help screens or printed guides to the database, or by altering the screen display so that full field labels are displayed instead of abbreviations.

Irrelevant Information

Some on-screen information is irrelevant to your needs, and it is often difficult to distinguish between relevant and irrelevant information.

On-Screen Information that Is Always Relevant: As a rule, any basic bibliographic information that appears on screen is always relevant. This includes the name of the author(s); any titles (of books, articles, journals, conferences, etc.); publication dates; and volume, issue, and page numbers. For books, place of publication is always relevant, as is conference location for published conference proceedings.

On-Screen Information that Is Sometimes Relevant: Call number and/or location information is relevant only if the call number and/or location information applies to a library you can use. For example, if the GPO database gives you Superintendent of Documents call numbers and your local government document collection uses Superintendent of Documents call numbers, then this information can be useful to you. However, if the Agricola database gives you National Agriculture Library call numbers and your library doesn't use NAL call numbers, then this information is unlikely to be useful to you. Similarly, if you use the Internet to call up a library on the other side of the world, the call number and location information you get is not going to help you.

Availability

In most electronic databases, information about availability means availability from a specific library or from a specific information vendor.

> Example: If an on-screen message tells you that something is unavailable from University Microfilms Incorporated, it doesn't mean that it isn't available in your local library.

Accession Numbers

Electronic databases often display accession numbers and other "record keeping" numbers. For the average user, these numbers are not important. A common exception to this rule are numbers (such as ERIC Document numbers) that correspond to microformat collections. These numbers are important if you have access to the microformat collection in question.

PRINTING AND DOWNLOADING

Most electronic databases allow you to print and/or download the information you retrieve.

MARKING RECORDS

Many electronic databases allow you to mark selected records for printing or downloading. This usually involves going through your search results one by one and pressing a key to mark those records you would like to print or download. The key you press to mark a record varies from database to database, but some common marking keys are **enter, space bar, tab, m, Alt-m,** or one of the function keys.

CUSTOMIZING RECORDS

Some electronic databases allow you to customize what parts of the records are printed or downloaded, i.e., print/download only citation, only abstracts, full-text without the citation, and so on.

LIMITS ON PRINTING/DOWNLOADING

Some electronic databases have limits on the number of records that can be printed and/or downloaded. Typically, individual libraries set print limits on the electronic databases they make available to the public. For some electronic databases there may be a fee based on the number of records you print or download. Some electronic databases allow you to print or download only one screen of information at a time. Most modern software has some sort of "capture" program that, when activated, automatically downloads everything that appears on the screen to a file on your computer's hard drive.

GETTING YOUR HANDS ON THE INFORMATION

BIBLIOGRAPHIC DATABASES

Many electronic databases are bibliographic databases—they tell you that a piece of information exists and give you what you need to identify it uniquely, but often they do not tell you where you can find that piece of information. Bibliographic databases usually are not related to the holdings of any particular library— they tell you what's been published in a particular subject area or in a prescribed set of periodicals. When working with such databases you need to write down, print, or download the bibliographic information and then use the resources of your local library to see if the information is available. Some bibliographic electronic databases are "linked" to the material owned by a particular library. These databases—typically periodical indexes— not only give you bibliographic information, they also tell you if the library they are linked to owns the piece of information and give you location information—which library or libraries the information is in and the call number under which it can be found.

Online library catalogs are bibliographic databases devoted to the holdings of a particular library or group of libraries. The fact that book, journal, or other type of information is cataloged in an online library catalog almost always means that it is owned by the library or libraries in question. Online catalogs also supply location information.

FULL-TEXT DATABASES

Some electronic databases are full-text, meaning whole units of information can be displayed on screen and downloaded or printed. Full-text databases often contain periodical articles, but some contain such things as legal documents, college catalogs, financial reports, encyclopedia articles, dictionary definitions, or the addresses and phone numbers of persons or businesses. Full-text databases with address-and-phone-number type information are often called **directory databases.**

DOCUMENT DELIVERY

Some bibliographic electronic databases, such as CARL UnCover, offer you the option of ordering the full text of any items your searches retrieve. There is usually a fee involved for such document-delivery services.

ENDING A SEARCH

There are a variety of ways to log out of an electronic database when you have finished a search or want to start searching in a different database. Pressing the Escape key will sometimes end a search session. Generally, when you press the Escape key the database prompts you to do something else (type *yes,* type *q,* etc.) to end your session. In many other electronic databases, and on the Internet, the Escape key will not end your search session. Some common commands for ending a session include:

- Quit
- Bye
- Stop
- Exit
- End
- Logoff
- Logout
- Q (for quit)
- D (for disconnect)
- F-10
- ^]

- ^c
- ^q
- alt-x (use this only as a last resort)

Some databases have time-out functions so that a search session ends automatically if no keys are pressed over a certain period of time. Help screens or other on-screen information will sometimes tell you the preferred way to end a session. When you are logging on to an electronic database you have never used before, keep your eyes open for information on how to get out of the database. Often this information comes at the beginning of a search and is not repeated later on—when you most need it.

5 INTRODUCING NEW USERS TO THE INTERNET

Katherine T. Durack
New Mexico State University

FIRST THINGS FIRST: TEACHING WHAT THE INTERNET IS

What is the Internet? Ask five people and you'll likely get five different descriptions—it's a situation similar to the old tale about the five blind men and the elephant. The problem is that it is always difficult to introduce any new technology and where the Internet is concerned, this problem is compounded by at least three factors:

- The changing variety of network names—the NREN, the Internet, the information superhighway, and the NII to name just a few.
- The alphabet soup of terms that identify technical features of the network (ftp, tcp/ip, etc.).
- The invisibility of the infrastructure that makes computer network communications possible.

Add to this the fact that different people use different services and benefits available via the Internet and it can be difficult to know where to begin. There are some characteristics, however, that most experienced Internet users share:

- "Net surfers" can typically picture "the Net" (metaphorically or otherwise).
- They have command of a vocabulary to describe the Net.
- They have a feeling for how the Net "works," i.e., they have some grasp of the social rules that apply to network interactions.

For new Internet users to become comfortable with the Internet, they will also need to be able to "see," describe, and understand the Net in addition to acquiring basic skills with network tools such as Gopher, Archie, and Mosaic. This chapter suggests ways that you can introduce the Internet to new users, offers specific suggestions for addressing common beginners' fears, and concludes with a few tips for helping new users evaluate information they might retrieve from the Net.

SEEING THE NET

"How does my E-mail message get from New Mexico to New Zealand?" Inevitably, new users want to know how messages get from one location to another. They want to know the details: how their message travels from the computer in this room to a computer in New Zealand. Asking about how messages get from point A to point B is a natural part of the learning process and one way users begin to build their mental model of the Net. Unfortunately, this may be the hardest need for teachers to meet. The physical infrastructure that supports network communications is geographically dispersed and even local portions of the hardware tend to be hidden away in closets, behind walls, and locked away in other buildings. The network cable connecting to the computer—that resembles any other cable—is about all that there is that you can show your students in the classroom. Beyond that, there's little else students can easily see. There are, however, some ideas and images you can bring into the classroom that will help new users build their own mental models.

Given the Internet's historical association with the United States Department of Defense (DOD) through DARPA (Defense Advanced Research Project), it's not surprising that transmission routes would be set up to be flexible: should one site be "neutralized" (to use a DOD euphemism for "bombed"), messages and data would naturally need to take another route to keep lines of communications open.

Students should learn to recognize that knowing the route is irrelevant. If a computer is down somewhere between New Mexico and New Zealand, messages will take an alternate route. Point out to students that most people are quite comfortable using the telephone and the postal service without knowing exactly how calls or letters go from one point to another. If new users can accept the Net as a kind of message-and-data delivery system similar to the telephone industry and the postal service, they may decide knowing the route is not so important after all and be better able to leave the technical details to technicians.

Find out typical paths messages from your area to elsewhere might take. One common structure for networks to take is a tree- or river-like hierarchy: small collections of computers are connected together locally into networks; local area networks may feed into regional networks; regional networks feed into larger networks and so forth. For example, at this writing my network access is provided through New Mexico State University's campus network, NMSU-Net. New Mexico State University (and others entities in the southwestern United States) are connected to each other in a larger, regional network, WESTNET. WESTNET, along with other regional networks, connects to the NSFNET, the United States' Internet "backbone." Via NSFNET, Internet users in the United States connect with other networks around the world. Of course, as the transmission technology changes, these hierarchies will change and may completely disappear—but having some idea of how the system works at present and how it has worked in the past can be helpful.

Try to obtain some network graphics. When it comes to trying to describe the Internet, a picture really is worth a thousand words, so when you're asking your local Net gurus about how messages and data originating from your site are transmitted elsewhere, be sure to ask if they have any graphics depicting local and regional networks. Because there are many different kinds of network diagrams and schematics (many of which are unintelligible to the average citizen), try to get images that have recognizable features, such as cities, states, and other familiar geographical boundaries. Look for images of network connectivity at the national and international level from is.internic.net in the about-internet/maps directory.

Use metaphors and draw analogies to help students create mental images. Using metaphors and drawing analogies are other means for helping new Net users come to understand the Net. The most common metaphor in use today is probably the "information superhighway," which draws upon a comparison between our roadway system as local and national conduits for goods and services. As indicated earlier, there are also parallels to the postal service and the cable television and telephone industries (in fact, boundaries between these entities are somewhat artificial and experts predict the eventual mergers of these currently separate industries). Another metaphor you might experiment with is the ocean, which Merit Network, Inc. developed in 1992 for its Internet training materials (both are vast, shared resources which have treasures and hazards). And don't overlook the term "network" for ideas—it is itself metaphoric, with allusions to the netting fishermen use to reap the bounties of the seas.

When you are looking for ways to explain the Internet, remember that a good analogy will have three features: something familiar, something unfamiliar, and a connection that links the two. The connection is the most vital aspect, and ideally will be something learners can immediately relate to in their own experience. For example, thinking of the network as an ocean may be effective for people who live in coastal areas or near other large bodies of water, but for desert dwellers the connection will be more abstract: the idea of the net will coincide only with an idea about the ocean. Stronger analogies will draw on situations or circumstances that learners have actually experienced: for desert dwellers, the desert itself may be a richer, more personal, and more vital metaphor. Deserts, after all, have oases, may also be vast, and similarly have hazards and hidden treasures.

WHAT'S IN A NAME? ABOUT BASIC INTERNETWORKING VOCABULARY

Novice computer users typically will need an introduction to the technology that includes some networking vocabulary. Exactly how much vocabulary you'll have to introduce will depend to some extent on the skill level of your class, the amount of information you plan to cover, and the specific network tools you plan to teach.

Glossaries for common Internet-related terms and acronyms can be found at is.internic.net. Resources include RFC 1392, the Internet Users' Glossary put together by a working group of the Internet Engineering Task Force. The glossary is thorough and specific in its terms, and often very technical, but well worth having for yourself and for your more advanced users. Another excellent source for simple explanations of complex concepts is NorthWestNet's Internet Passport. For information on the Internet Passport send an E-mail to passport@nwnet.net.

Network terms are often hopelessly slippery and difficult for learners to grasp. You will likely need to develop your own list of necessary vocabulary based on the specific services available to your students. Good glossaries are readily available, electronically and in print (see above), so rather than adding to the plenitude of interpretations this chapter will attempt to provide some insight into why new learners often find the terminology very difficult to master. There are some very good reasons for confusion about Internet terminology, and you might want to share these with your class.

Some terms describe things that exist; yet similar terms describe only ideas and political agendas. Take for example the common terms used to describe the Internet: the internet, the information superhighway, and the National Information Infrastructure (NII). The Internet names a concrete reality: it has physical components, a history, and working social and administrative structures. In contrast, the terms information superhighway and NII are terms which describe ideas and political agendas; while these ideas are based on the current Internet and the way it works, they are not necessarily one and the same, but rather reflect conceptions of the future of the Internet.

Network-ese, like bureaucratese and government-ese, relies a great deal on acronyms. Given the Net's original association with government organizations, it's not surprising that network nomenclature would share some of the characteristics of bureaucratese. One readily apparent characteristic is the reliance on acronyms: tcp/ip, ftp, and so forth. There's no denying that in certain communities acronyms play a vital communicative function, providing a meaningful shorthand for the technologically expert; the problem lies in the use of such terms to describe the kinds of activities any network users—novice and expert alike—might like to use. Unfortunately, in many cases unpacking the acronyms—stating, for example, that tcp/ip stands for transmission control protocol/Internet protocol—will only add to the confusion.

Network nomenclature is idiosyncratic; there is often no discernible or intuitive reason why something was given a particular name. For example, at least two E-mail packages have adopted names of trees (pine and elm) and yet another uses an old-fashioned female name (Eudora), while Archie (along with Jughead and Veronica) are named for a comic strip, and have to do with searching ftp sites. The language describing network activities that aren't associated with programs is colorful as well, e.g., flaming (heated electronic exchanges or insults) and lurking (observing electronic interactions without making yourself known).

Many terms are both nouns and verbs, often naming software and describing activity: Also, perhaps due to inheritance from bureaucratese, there is the tendency for nouns to become verbs, as in *interface* and *to interface, ftp* and *to ftp, Gopher* and *to Gopher, Telnet* and *to Telnet,* and so forth. Clarifying this with your students—explaining that Telnet is both a software name and the activity you do with the software—should help them as they come across written instructions for using the Net in the classroom, in publications, and in electronic discussions.

APPROPRIATE USE AND NETIQUETTE

Appropriate use and "netiquette" are two topics any class on network use should address. Exactly what "appropriate use" is may be determined for you locally: computer centers often publish usage guidelines—the ground rules that specify the kinds of activities that are generally acceptable, suspect, or forbidden. Rules differ from site to site and may vary widely. For instance, MUDs and MOOs ("multi-user dimension" and "MUD object oriented," kinds of electronic, word-based virtual reality) may be forbidden or restricted at some universities because these activities are considered by the particular rule-makers as frivolous and wasteful of system resources, whereas other, more system-intensive activities are sanctioned. It's worth noting, however, that some writing researchers expect MUDs and MOOs to have a unique pedagogical value, and that some corporations have established MUDs and MOOs for worker recreation, so whether they are "good" or "bad" is a judgment that lies clearly in the eyes of the beholder.

If your site does not publish an acceptable use policy, you may want to introduce your learners to the "Bill of Rights and Responsibilities for the Electronic Community of Learners," published in August 1993 by EDUCOM. The product of two years of discussion and collaboration among members of the academic community, this document strives to balance the sometimes conflicting attitudes of electronic resource users and the administrative entities which oversee them.

To learn more about EDUCOM write to 1112 Sixteenth Street, NW, Suite 600, Washington, D.C. 20036. For more information about the Bill of Rights and Responsibilities Project, contact Frank Connolly at the American University (frank@ american.edu).

Similar to acceptable use policies, appropriate netiquette is often situationally determined and not universal among different social entities on the Net. Usenet news, for instance, has published two guides advising participants in the rules and manners expected of participants. In practice, adherence to the rules varies widely, but "Emily Postnews Answers Your Questions on Netiquette" and "Rules for Posting to Usenet" should help keep new Usenet users from making terrible social gaffes. (Both documents are published regularly on the Usenet newsgroup news.announce.newusers.) Other electronic social gatherings—Listservs, MUDs, and MOOs, etc.—generally provide new participants with some sort of purpose statement and guideline for participation. Encourage net learners to read and follow the advice in these documents, at least until they become accustomed to how a particular group works.

Emoticons, or "smileys," help make up for the lack of visual cues that sometimes impairs or influences electronic interactions. The "Unofficial Smiley Dictionary" (available from is.internic.net) will provide your class with a humorous introduction to the creative ways net users have tried to overcome the limitations of text-based electronic communication. (Note, however, that the meanings of some of the more obscure smileys may be lost on some users.)

TYPICAL NEW USERS' FEARS AND WAYS TO ADDRESS THEM

In teaching people to use the Internet, you can anticipate encountering some common kinds of fears and misconceptions. Some that have been encountered are listed below, with ideas for addressing them.

"I DON'T KNOW WHERE TO START."

Many novice net users, particularly those who are relatively new to computers, may become easily overwhelmed with the Net. Somehow learning about the Net seems to be too much, too fast, and more than they can possibly remember. Address this concern by:

- Introducing new concepts slowly and carefully.
- Reviewing old concepts before going on to new ideas.
- Offering plenty of in-class practice time.
- Introducing services that are relevant to the individual (for example, introducing public school teachers to the ongoing conversations in the Usenet news K12 hierarchy or K12 Listservs).

"WHERE DO I GET HELP?"

New Net users will likely want a lot of help, and will tend to want to rely on the teacher as expert. As you introduce more and more people to the Net, this obviously has the potential to become quite a burden. Address this concern by:

- Using a buddy system, pairing new learners in teams.
- Identifying multiple sources for user assistance.
- Providing users with problems to solve in class.
- Emphasizing that it is unlikely any one person will ever have all the right answers, and the Net provides an opportunity to ask a lot of people outside of the user's own locale.

"HOW DO I GET A LIST OF SERVICES?"

New users typically want some sort of list of all the services they can access via the Internet, and many book retailers are happy to comply—the only problem is that the Net is mercurial in nature and few things on the Net are static. Address this concern by:

- Explaining that the dynamic nature of the Net is both a liability and a benefit (there's more available every day).
- Allowing users to do some in-class electronic exploration of their own.
- Demonstrating how you might use the Net to find out where or whether or not a service exists.

"I'LL NEVER BE ABLE TO DO THIS BY MYSELF."

New net users are often concerned they'll never be able to use the tools they're learning or learn to navigate the Internet themselves. Address this concern by providing:

- Plenty of in-class practice.
- Step-by-step documentation for each of the tools they will be learning.
- A structure for peer support (a buddy system).
- Phone numbers for your local computer/network assistance line.

"I'M AFRAID I'LL BREAK A COMPUTER IN KALAMAZOO."

Once they've successfully connected to a computer in another location, new users may be afraid they'll forget the right commands and do something (in their attempts to explore or disconnect from the remote source) that will damage the remote computer. Address this concern by assuring users that:

- Given the Internet's 25-year history lots of people have explored and improperly exited from remote hosts with little or no ill effects.
- Most system administrators will insist that systems which are accessible online are able to withstand user errors.

"I'LL GET PERMANENTLY STUCK ONLINE."

Few systems maintain an on-screen prompt indicating to users how to exit properly once they're done exploring. Address this concern by:

- Recommending users always have pen and paper handy to jot down messages displayed when connecting to a remote host.
- Providing users with a list of common exit strategies. For instance, ctrl-] q works on many systems, and common logoff commands include q, quit, close, logoff, logout, exit, and bye.

- Figuring out worst-case scenarios and telling users what happens if they simply give up and turn the power off. With some systems, users may be left logged on and need to call someone in order to log back in again. Also note that if users are dialing in to a remote host via a modem, just shutting down the software may not be enough to break the telephone connection; to force the connection closed, some users must turn the modem off or pick up the telephone.

"I'LL CATCH A COMPUTER VIRUS."

"Catching" and spreading computer viruses is a legitimate risk that goes along with using diskettes in more than one computer and with using networks. Address this concern by:

- Educating users about computer viruses, including worst-case scenarios.
- Documenting and practicing practical safeguards (such as keeping back-up diskettes and running virus-checkers on downloaded files).
- Providing users with information on how to obtain anti-virus software for their own computers.
- Using anti-virus software in the teaching environment (discuss how it is set up and why; demonstrate what happens if a virus is found).

If you need to find out more on computer viruses, you can subscribe to the VIRUS-L Listserv (send the message SUB VIRUS-L your-name to LISTSERV@LEHIGH.EDU) or read the comp.virus newsgroup available on Usenet news (they're the same thing). Or you can FTP the virus FAQs from cert.org (look in the pub/virus-l directory).

"IT'LL COST ME A FORTUNE."

Some teachers notice that learners are timid in their approach to the Net because the costs of networking are often not readily discernible to the individual. While some individuals do pay for Internet access through local service providers, others may have "free" access through educational organizations, community networks, and libraries. In the extreme, either view—that the Net is a free resource, or that the Net is some kind of sneaky 900 number—can be problematic. In the former case, do remind learners they are using a shared resource, and in the case of free access through schools, that may mean strictly recreational use should be curbed to ensure that appropriate educational uses can take place. (Obviously, one can argue about the boundaries between recreational and educational activities and the politics of sanctioned and unsanctioned use, but, whatever your beliefs, it is useful to know local policy.) With regard to fearful learners, you might remind them that taxpayer dollars have paid for the resource to a great extent, and will likely continue to be involved in its expansion and future development. In this sense I suppose it is rather like a sneaky 900 number, but it is at least one which should strike individual pocketbooks more or less uniformly and then only once a year.

"THE NETWORK MARKS THE END OF CIVILIZATION AS WE KNOW IT."

Certainly there are people who hold this opinion, and it is true that technologies often shape our social interactions and our lifestyles. Whether or not the network will have the sweeping effects some expect is a story for time to tell, and judging from the pace at which new technologies are introduced each day, some inkling of how things will shake out during the next decade or so will become apparent. I doubt, however, that computer networks have the potential to change human nature but they may change the structure of many of our interactions.

"THE NETWORK IS THE SOURCE FOR ALL MY INFORMATION NEEDS."

At least at this writing, this just isn't the case, but the network is a marvelous source for all kinds of facts and opinions. Yet your students may notice that in many electronic information seeking forays they will be referred to other sources—books, articles, radio, and TV—as well as to sources on the Net. In fact, some discussion groups will become outright testy if they think someone who hasn't done their homework is using the Net as a quick and easy way to get someone to do their searching for them.

GEMS AND JUNK: TIPS FOR EVALUATING INFORMATION RETRIEVED FROM THE NETWORK

Novice network users—like many television viewers—may easily fall into the trap of taking everything they read, see, or retrieve from the Net as THE TRUTH. Point out to students that almost anyone with a computer and a connection can "publish" whatever they want to on the Net. The lack of gatekeepers—one function of the print-based publishing community—has both advantages and disadvantages. On the good side, people have access to ideas and information that otherwise might be unavailable; on the other hand, no one entity is responsible for verifying facts and evaluating the usefulness of files to ensure any standard of quality, so there is a lot of junk out there in addition to the gems. Encourage your students to apply the same kinds of evaluative skills they would use with any other medium (conversations, books, radio, and television) to the Net.

> Some good sources for information pertaining to the Internet itself are the Electronic Frontier Foundation (eff.org) for information on legislation pertaining to electronic privacy and individual rights; EDUCOM (educom.edu), which focuses on issues pertaining to education and computing; and the InterNIC (is.internic.net), a provider of Internet information services.

Consider the source. Some sites and high-profile Net users gradually develop reputations based on the kinds of information (or garbage) they produce. Even sites with good reputations (such as those listed in the boxed text) will likely have an agenda or a point of view that site owners support. Information from a stranger should be considered just that—information from a stranger.

Confirm with the source and get a second opinion. If information gathered from the network will affect decisions you'll make or actions you'll take, be certain you and your students check facts with other sources. As experienced Net users recognize, there are folk tales that new users often act on, such as the propagation of the $150 cookie recipe and the post cards for a poor sick child. Alert students to such lore, and encourage them to check their facts with the named source or parties involved and to get second opinions on important information.

Double-check the data and the date. While it's fairly easy to make documents available to people via the Internet, it's a lot harder to keep them updated and current. Many documents will have "last updated" dates on them, and users should be aware that just because it came off the Net, that doesn't mean something is fresh, new, current, and complete.

Stop, look, and listen. If you subscribe to the information superhighway metaphor, it makes sense to apply some street sense: stop, look, and listen before entering the on-ramp or crossing the road. Most of the previous advice can be summarized with these few words learned as children.

USING THE INTERNET TO TEACH THE INTERNET

M. Marlo Brown
New Mexico State University Library

Information to assist Internet teachers can come from many sources. A wealth of books about the Internet has been published, and more articles on the subject are written every day. Some of the best and most up-to-date material, however, is available on the Internet itself. You merely need to know where to look.

Instructional materials exist on the Internet in a variety of forms. There are books, conference papers, journal articles, essays, FAQs (Frequently Asked Questions pertaining to a particular topic), online workshops and seminars, news releases, and much more. Information can also be gleaned from Internet discussion groups of various types. It is vital, however, to remember the nature of the Internet. It is a chaotic, unsupervised, and ever-changing entity. That wonderful Internet resource you find today may disappear tomorrow. Although it sometimes seems that the more useful a resource is the quicker it disappears from the Net, new resources are always becoming available. In fact, the greatest failing of many published Internet books is that rather than giving an overall understanding of what is available on the Internet, they instead show a snapshot of what was available before the book went to press.

BOOKS, ESSAYS, AND OTHER DOCUMENTS

Text files, such as books, conference papers, essays, and other publications are easily available to most people with access to the Internet. Many pioneers in Internet teaching and exploration have created guides to the Internet that are available on the Internet in various locations. These works include explanations of Internet tools, lists of excellent Internet resources, reports of new resources available on the Net, and other useful information.

The classic book about cyberspace is *Zen and the Art of the Internet* by Brendan P. Kehoe. The latest edition can be purchased in bookstores, but the first edition (1992) has been out on the Internet for some time. Although it is somewhat dated, it is still a good source of information for Internet explorers and trainers. It is also one of the most common Internet text files and can be found in dozens of locations throughout the world.

Other classic Internet text files include *The Big Dummy's Guide to the Internet* and *The Hacker's Dictionary,* both of which can be found in many sites. *The Big Dummy's Guide to the Internet* was created by Apple Computer, Inc. and the Electronic Frontier Foundation. Intended as an introduction to the Internet for beginners, it includes extensive information on initially connecting to the Net as well as brief how-to essays on everything from Archie to UNIX. As with any text file, it has aged somewhat, but it is still a useful resource and a good example of one attempt to teach the Internet in a single lesson. *The Hacker's Dictionary,* also known as *The Jargon File,* is a glossary of the language of the hacker counterculture. Many of these terms have found their way into general usage on the Internet, especially in some of the Usenet newsgroups. Fun to browse, *The Hacker's Dictionary* can also be useful in introducing beginners to one of the many subcultures present on the Internet.

Zen and the Art of the Internet and other text files can be found in a variety of ways. The easiest, if the title is known, is simply to perform a filename search on Archie to check File Transfer Protocol (FTP) sites, or a keyword search with Veronica, Jughead, or other search software to look for the file in Gophers. Remember, however, that Archie searches for filenames and that the title of a file may be an alternate or abbreviated form of the title of the original work. Using part of the title can be useful with Archie. The word "zen," for example, is an effective Archie search term for finding a text-file version of Brendan Kehoe's book.

Some of the most useful text files on the Internet are quietly created by individuals or groups and made available to the Internet community at large. Scott Yanoff's list of Internet resources (which can be found on many sites on the Internet) is an outstanding example of this type of individual effort. As with all other resources on the Net, text files can come and go without warning. For this reason, it is best to download a useful file, mail it to yourself, make a printout, or save it in some other manner in case it disappears soon after discovery. Few things are more frustrating than encountering a wonderful article somewhere on the Internet and then never being able to find it again.

Text files can be stored in a variety of formats, but the most common is a plain text format known as ASCII (pronounced as'-

kee). Text files are commonly downloaded to your home machine via FTP, although Gophers and World Wide Web (WWW) browsers are also being used for this purpose. While Gopher and WWW offer easier downloading, FTP can provide access to text files at sites that cannot be reached via Gopher or WWW.

HELP FILES

Some of the best explanations of resources and how to use them can be found in the help files scattered throughout the Internet. Online help files often contain clear, concise descriptions and/or instructions that are of great assistance in teaching others how to use a system. The better help files were created by the system experts and offer excellent summaries of useful commands. The Internet Gopher help files are a good example of this. They can be activated at any time while connected to a Gopher. You merely press the <?> key to read a very complete list of commands for Gopher navigation, for using Gopher bookmarks, etc.

Another source of helpful information is found in the summary that often accompanies an Internet resource. WWW homepages, Gopher menus, bulletin boards, FTP sites, and other complex Internet tools and systems frequently contain some sort of explanatory file which tells a new user where things are, how the resource is organized, who to contact with problems, etc. When you log into a system, a help file generally appears on the first screen or is at least mentioned among the first words to scroll across the screen. To find a help file look for words such as **readme, readme, about this system,** etc. Because of the time help files can save, even experienced Internet users are in the habit of looking for them when checking out a new system or resource. They can also be a good starting point for creating Internet teaching materials.

GOPHERS

Gophers—with their layers of menus—lend themselves to finding helpful Internet resources. An excellent tactic is to use some of the larger, better known Gophers as starting points for exploration. Many of these Gophers provide links to valuable resources in other systems—links which are kept up to date by groups of experienced Internet users. At the time of this writing, some of the more useful Gophers for Internet resource information include:

Library of Congress Gopher— LC Marvel	marvel.loc.gov
National Library of Canada Gopher Server (English Version)	gopher.nlc-bnc.ca
RiceInfo (Rice University, Houston, TX)	riceinfo.rice.edu
University of Michigan Libraries	gopher.lib.umich.edu

Archie, Veronica, and other Internet searching tools can be used to find known items, but learning about new resources can be challenging. A method that sometimes is successful is just searching random keywords with Veronica or Jughead. When looking for Internet materials on nursing, for example, a search with the keyword "nursing" in Veronica gives a wealth of useful resources. Text files can be found in a number of different forms on the Internet and in a variety of locations. The easiest—and often most successful—method of finding out about helpful resources for Internet trainers is through other people on the Net. There is far more out there than users can keep up with on their own, so it makes sense to use the Internet to communicate with others who have similar interests. (See the section on Listservs and Usenet below.)

WORLD WIDE WEB

WWW sites can be reached with Mosaic, Lynx, or other Internet "Web browsing" software packages. For Internet teachers, Mosaic, Netscape, and other graphic interfaces can be a great way to grab the attention of an audience. They offer a combination of different types of text and graphics ranging from simple line drawings to high-resolution photographs. Mosaic's graphics, however, can slow even the fastest machine down to crawling speed, especially during hours of peak use. Although they may not be ideal for WWW demonstrations in all cases, graphical Web browsers, in addition to text-based browsers, should be used to look at a WWW site before recommending it to new users.

The greatest challenge for an Internet trainer in using WWW is finding the resources. At this time, WWW does not offer searching software similar to that used to search Gophers. For this reason, WWW users are dependent upon word of mouth to find out about new and useful Web sites. As with many Internet resources, new WWW locations are often announced on Listservs and Usenet newsgroups. The other way to find new Web resources is to follow the links set up in existing WWW sites. Many creators of Web "homepages" attempt to locate and provide links to other interesting and useful WWW resources.

Web resources, as opposed to Gophers, can be created easily by an individual with limited computer experience. For this reason, WWW is, in many cases, very specialized and offers access to unique information that is available nowhere else on the Internet. It also means that Web resources can be extremely volatile. As with other Internet information, it is best to write down, print, or otherwise save the location information about any useful WWW resource that you plan to visit in the future. The link which allowed you to connect to the site on Monday may not exist on Tuesday.

One source which regularly announces information about new WWW and Gopher sites is InterNIC's Scout Report. The Scout Report is a weekly announcement which you can subscribe to by sending the message **subscribe scout-report** to **majordomo@ is.internic.net**. The Scout Report is also accessible via Gopher.

LISTSERVS AND USENET

Listservs (mailing List Services) and Usenet newsgroups offer Internet teachers a forum for trying out new ideas, reading about the experiences of others, and asking questions about resources, documentation, teaching techniques, etc. Usenet newsgroups and Listserv mailing lists are also where many new and/or updated Internet resources are announced. There seem to be Listservs on almost every conceivable topic, but some of these are also available via Usenet. For busy professionals, Usenet newsgroups offer the advantage of messages that can be viewed when time is available. Listservs, on the other hand, can fill up an electronic mail in-box with messages which must be regularly deleted. As with other Internet resources, Listservs and newsgroups can come and go frequently; the groups listed here are subject to change without warning.

It is highly recommended that Usenet beginners start by reading the newsgroup **news.announce.newusers** for general information on Usenet. Tutorials and essays concerning Usenet newsgroups frequently appear there and often include information on posting messages, newsgroup etiquette, how to start your own newsgroup, etc. It is also a good source of information for teachers of Usenet. Also good is **news.newusers.questions**, where new users of Usenet and/or the Internet have a chance to ask the most basic questions without being "flamed" by impatient, more experienced Net users. This newsgroup can be an excellent source for learning the problems that some new users of the Internet are facing.

At the time of this writing, one of the best discussion groups for Internet teachers is available as both a Usenet newsgroup and as a Listserv. Nettrain is the Network Trainers List, and it covers a wide variety of topics pertaining to teaching people to use the Internet and other networks. On Usenet, it appears as **bit.listserv.nettrain**. Other potentially useful Usenet newsgroups include:

alt.internet. services	This newsgroup contains questions and answers on Internet resources of various types, Internet tools, new Net access points, and software packages for Internet access. It is, however, sometimes overrun with new users looking for free Internet access from a particular location.
alt.best.of. internet	A newsgroup created for the posting of Internet "gems" found elsewhere.
alt.bbs. internet	This is a discussion of bulletin board systems available through the Internet. It is often a mix of new free-access Bulletin Board Systems (BBS) announcements and ads for commercial BBSs.
comp.internet. net-happenings	This newsgroup is one of the best places to find out about new Gophers, WWW sites, online journals and newsletters, etc.
news.announce. conferences	Announcements of upcoming conferences and calls for papers.
news.announce. newgroups	This newsgroup posts announcements of new and proposed Usenet groups as well as announcements about superseded, cancelled, and bogus newsgroups.
news.lists	Look here for listings of the thousands of available Listservs and Usenet newsgroups.

The best starting point for any newsgroup is the FAQ file.

FAQs try to answer many of the basic questions about a group, and some also describe the types of questions/discussions that are appropriate for the newsgroup. By reading the FAQ, a person who is new to a newsgroup can avoid the embarrassment of being "flamed" for bringing up a topic that's been discussed many times on the newsgroup. Some of the better FAQs are quite long and give a large amount of excellent information on a variety of topics. Some newsgroups even go so far as having separate FAQs for detailed treatment of specialized subjects. For example, an Internet trainer or student wanting to know more about downloading graphics or sending graphics to people over the Internet could turn to the **alt.binaries.pictures** FAQ, which appears regularly on **alt.binaries.pictures.d** (the discussion newsgroup for those who use the Internet to post or download pictures of various types) as well as in the **news.answers** newsgroup. This FAQ describes how people can exchange pictures over the Internet, including the rules of etiquette to follow when posting or downloading graphics files. FAQs similar to this one can serve as a starting point for instructing new Usenet users. As a general rule, FAQs are periodically posted to the newsgroup that they were created for, and can also be found on a regular basis in **news.answers**, a Usenet newsgroup that serves as a repository for FAQs and similar documents.

ONLINE WORKSHOPS AND OTHER ACTIVITIES

With the availability of Usenet newsgroups and Listservs, the Internet can easily convey information to a large number of people at one time. Thus it was natural that the Internet would eventually be used as a distance-education tool. What better way to teach large numbers of people all over the world how to use the Internet than with the Internet itself? Online workshops are a wonderful way for someone with basic knowledge of the Internet to learn more about tools they haven't used, and, with careful supervision, such workshops can be used to help train new users who have minimal online skills and experience.

A good example of an online Internet workshop is the "Navigating the Internet: Let's Go Gopherin'" series sent out over the Net by Richard Smith of the Carnegie Library of Pittsburgh and Jim Gerland of the State University of New York at Buffalo. The workshop consists of a series of lessons sent to subscribers by electronic mail, and it teaches about Gophers on several levels, ranging from basic commands for users to information on setting up and running a Gopher server. Workshop announcements are generally posted in appropriate Usenet newsgroups and Listservs, and the workshops themselves may also be archived at one or more anonymous FTP sites. For example, Let's Go Gopherin' can still be found on many Internet sites.

Other types of Internet activities include newsletters, electronic journals, and contests. Because electronic mail files allow you to send a message to a large group of people at one stroke, many people have started sending out their own newsletters. With no mailing costs and very little work involved in distribution, almost anyone can create his or her own Internet newsletter. Some of these are simply collections or reprints of materials gathered either on the Internet or from regular print media. Others, however, are original publications. As one might expect, many newsletters distributed over the Internet deal with computers, telecommunications, and other topics of interest to Net users and Internet teachers. Examples of useful Internet newsletters include *NetCetera,* a quarterly publication describing new Internet tools and resources; the *Internet Monthly Report,* published by the Internet Research Group; and the *Online Chronicle of Distance Education and Communication.* For those who have a copy of the *Big Dummy's Guide to the Internet,* there is a monthly update of the guide distributed as a newsletter.

Newsletters and electronic magazines ("e-zines") can also provide a view into the world of the fringe culture of the Internet. Self-styled "cyberpunks," "hackers," "crackers," "phone phreaks" and others use such publications to share ideas and information with one another and to brag about past escapades. Some e-zines, such as *Line Noiz,* are useful to Internet trainers for the different perspective that they provide, while others, such as *Voices from the Net,* can be a source of useful information about little-known Internet resources and systems. Many who refer to themselves as hackers do not commit crimes with computers but rather explore the limits of computer systems' capabilities. They can be a source of information on features and shortcuts not mentioned in software documentation. As with any gray literature, however, information from any newsletter or e-zine must be taken with a grain of salt, and new resources or new ways of doing things should be thoroughly tested and explored before they are taught to new users or included in handouts or other publications.

Finding newsletters and e-zines can be difficult, as they are often not advertised at all or go out only to the members of a particular organization. Professional contacts, Listservs and Usenet newsgroups, and word of mouth from friends may be the only way of discovering these elusive but potentially valuable gray publications. The ARL (Association of Research Libraries) produces, at the time of this writing, a set of directories of online newsletters and electronic journals. These directories are made available both in print and in an abridged form over the Internet.

Internet contests can be a surprisingly fun way to learn about new information sources on the Internet. One of the best known is the Internet Hunt. Organized by Rick Gates of the University of Arizona, the Hunt consists of ten questions sent out on a monthly basis. The questions cover the full range of Net resources and are rated from one to ten in difficulty. Players have one week to E-mail the answers to Rick Gates, with the first player to answer correctly all questions being declared the winner. Individual winners and team winners are announced.

Rick Gates believes that experience, as opposed to formal classroom instruction, is the best way to learn how to use the Internet. The Hunt gives users of the Internet an idea of the great range of resources available to them. When the answers to each Hunt are posted, they give beginners a chance to see how experienced Internet surfers look for the information. For participants, it gives practice in "real world" Net searching. At the time of this writing, the Internet Hunt is on a brief hiatus but is expected to start again in February of 1995. The Hunt can be found on a number of Gophers in the U.S. It also appears regularly on many of the library-oriented Listservs and on the Usenet **alt.bbs.internet** and **alt.internet.services** newsgroups. Of course, Internet trainers can create their own contests and distribute them to their students to teach the use of selected Internet resources.

CONCLUSIONS

The Internet offers the Internet trainer a variety of materials to use in training others to navigate cyberspace. In a never-ending state of change, the Internet's huge collection of resources is impossible to catalog fully. The volatility of many Internet resources suggests that they be downloaded, printed, or otherwise saved immediately after they are found, in case they are removed from the Net without warning. Finding and making use of new resources is a challenging task at best. A host of tools and methods can be used to locate useful Internet materials, but the most effective single method is communication with other Net users, whether in Listservs, Usenet newsgroups, or by some other means. The Internet is run and maintained by people, and people remain its most valuable source of information.

PUTTING TOGETHER AN ELECTRONIC INFORMATION LITERACY WORKSHOP

Valerie J. Horton
New Mexico State University Library

HOW TO START

The first questions to ask yourself when putting together an electronic literacy workshop is: who is your audience? In fact, this question should be asked at every stage in the planning process. If your focus remains on your audience, the result will be a successful workshop.

Ask yourself:

- What does your audience need?
- How does your audience learn?
- What mix of theory and how-to information should you present?
- How much experience have they had with electronic resources?
- Are they likely to have electronic mail (E-mail) accounts?
- Are they professional librarians, skilled clerical staff, or newcomers to libraries?

Principles of Adult Learning[1]

Law of Primacy: first and last impressions stay the longest with the adult learner.

Law of Exercise: the more an act is repeated, the more quickly it is established as a habit.

Law of Disuse: a skill not practiced will be lost or forgotten.

Law of Intensity: a vivid, dramatic, or exciting presentation will be remembered.

Once you have a clear idea who your audience is, the next step is to choose the workshop topic. Again, you want to fit your topic to your audience.

Ask yourself:

- Is there evidence of need or interest in the topic?
- Is the topic so new that potential participants won't have had ample opportunity to learn about it from some other source?
- Is the topic timely?
- Is the topic within the capacity of the organizers to handle successfully?
- Does the topic fit the mission of the sponsoring organization?

Potential electronic literacy workshop topics change constantly. There is likely to be an audience that fits every topic at every level of experience. Your challenge is timing your workshop so that it fits into your local environment.

Make sure you consider the resources of the sponsoring agency. Whether the agency is a junior high school, a university, or a library association, electronic literacy workshops require a substantial amount of resources. Make sure you have the full support and enthusiasm of your sponsoring agency before you begin.

GOAL SETTING

Once the audience and topic are clearly understood, the next step is to develop a goal based on a blending of audience needs and a timely topic. Goals are usually defined as desired results of an activity or an anticipated outcome. Goals should be stated in clear, short statements that can be used later in publicity flyers and on registration forms. When developing your goal be clear on what you want to accomplish. Goals associated with electronic literacy often involve developing skills in computer proficiency. An example of a goal for an electronic literacy workshop would be:

> Introduce school district library personnel to the Internet command Telnet. Using Telnet, participants will learn how to access local and national electronic resources.

Workshop goals often include the stated desire as in the example above, but also may include hidden goals. For instance, the desire to produce a positive attitude in school library employees about computer networks may be an unstated goal. It is all right to have an unadvertised goal, just make sure you are aware of it.

DEVELOPING OBJECTIVES

Once the overall goals are established, the next step is to develop workshop objectives. Objectives are developed by breaking the goal into manageable and measurable pieces.

The objective should specifically state that participants will:

- Acquire knowledge
- Gain abilities or skills
- Change attitudes and behaviors

You are going to use the objectives to plan out and, later, to evaluate the workshop. Spend enough time developing your objectives to make sure they are clear and measurable. The number of objectives will depend on the length of the workshop. As a rule of thumb, a half-day workshop would need two or three objectives while a full-day session could use as many as four or five.

An example of objectives for a half-day workshop on using the Telnet command would be:

- Participants should know what the Telnet command is and be able to recognize how the Telnet command fits into the Internet environment.
- Participants should be able to Telnet to regional libraries and search online catalogs.
- Participants should be able to access two or three national electronic resources across the Internet.

Developing objectives is a balancing act. Having too many objectives means you are presenting too much information which may lead to confusion. Having too few objectives means too little information is being imparted which may lead to boredom. Most workshop planners err on the side of presenting too much information. Ask yourself, is it better to have the participants really process and internalize new knowledge and feel prepared to use a new skill or to feel they have skimmed a broad topic and been introduced to skills they have not truly gained? You develop your objectives accordingly.

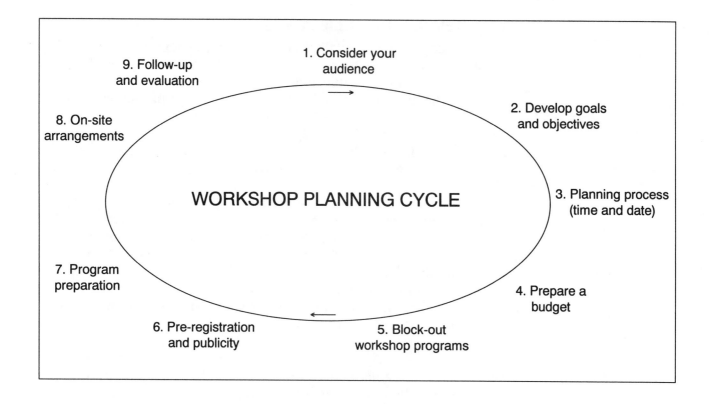

THE PLANNING PROCESS

Careful preplanning will greatly enhance the chances for your workshop's success. In fact, it's during the planning process that most of your decisions are made and the work of your willing helpers is coordinated. The planning process includes choosing a date and length, finding a facility, developing a workshop format, blocking out the programs, and anticipating costs.

HOW LONG?

How long should your workshop last? Obviously, the topic and the type of participants will be the major deciding factors. The Telnet command can be covered comprehensively in less than a half day. But another Internet command, File Transfer Protocol (FTP), could require a day or more.

Your audience will have a great impact on the length of your workshop. If your audience is limited to a local school district in a single metropolitan area, then a workshop during a class hiatus is appropriate. If your audience covers a large state, then you will need to time your workshop around driving distances and the possible need for a hotel stay. National workshops add exponentially to planning difficulties. The wider your audience base, the longer your planning process will take.

Once you have decided on the length of the workshop, you must choose a date. Choosing a date seems straightforward, and if you consider holidays, speaker availability, and give yourself plenty of lead time, you can minimize conflicts. However, choosing a date is invariably prone to hidden conflicts. If possible, check with organizations similar to your own to see if they have planned an event on or near the date of your workshop. The length of the workshop can also affect the date selected. A date for a half-day workshop can be selected with reasonable certainty that you know local conflicts, but a three-day national conference with an audience from multiple locations, cultures, and school schedules can be much more difficult to arrange.

WHERE WILL YOUR WORKSHOP TAKE PLACE?

The next step is to choose a facility for your workshop and to consider its convenience and accessibility. Determine if the facility is of the proper size, has adequate parking, access to lodging and restaurants, and, of course, is reasonably priced. Tour the facility first. Get a master plan with seating styles and numbers per room. Remember adults learn best in attractive, comfortable settings. Facilities that are too hot, too cold, or too noisy, will distract the audience.

Electronic literacy workshops have the added dimension of requiring that considerable attention be paid to equipment and connections. The facility may limit the number of terminals or PCs available per person during the training. Can the facility handle the specific equipment you need, i.e., MAC, DOS, or UNIX operating systems? Are there enough network connections or telephone lines with modems? Are computer projection panels, portable VCRs, overhead projectors, and marker boards available? What are the alternatives if any of the above equipment isn't available or doesn't work? Electronic literacy workshops require that equipment consideration be given top priority.

Facility Checklist

Are there electrical outlets, phone jacks, and network connections?

Is there a separate place for speakers to prepare?

Are there enough restrooms?

Are there auditoriums, large and small meeting rooms, and dividable rooms?

Are the tables and chairs adequate and comfortable?

Does noisy equipment operate near the conference room?

Is the temperature comfortable? Is it adjustable?

Are the rooms ventilated?

Is the light adequate? Can the room be darkened?

Is there a convenient break area for food and beverages?

Does the sound system work?

Is parking available?

Are there hotels, restaurants, convenience stores, gas stations, and hospitals nearby?

What will participants need to bring with them that is not provided at the facility?

DEVELOPING THE WORKSHOP FORMAT

There are a number of different formats for presenting sessions during the workshop. Some formats lend themselves better to electronic literacy workshops than others. Your objectives (and probably your facility) will serve as a guide in choosing the most suitable format.

SPEAKERS

Without question the most common session format is a speaker. While speakers are often overused, they can be quite dramatic and serve to frame and focus the entire workshop. In general, workshop planners have found that speakers are best when used at the beginning of a workshop as, for example, a keynote speaker; or for longer workshops, to break the workshop into logical subtopics. For best results make sure someone has heard the person give a public address prior to inviting him or her to speak at your workshop. For electronic literacy workshops, a speaker can be used to present the global picture. For instance, in our example of a Telnet workshop, the speaker could introduce the history and development of the Internet including information on the Telnet command.

PANELS

Panels are made up of several speakers usually speaking for a shorter time period than a single speaker. Panels work best when you want to be proactive or present contrasting points of views. For instance, a panel could address whether or not children should be allowed access to some of the adult materials available on the network. Always make sure you include time for audience response and continued discussion.

DEMONSTRATIONS

Demonstrations are a common session format found in electronic literacy workshops. An advantage of demonstrations is that adults are adept at imitating the behavior of experts. Unfortunately, an equally common reason for the use of demonstrations is that there are not enough computers for participants to have hands-on practice. Despite this drawback, demonstrations can be useful, particularly when used to introduce an electronic resource that is new to most of the audience.

HANDS-ON PRACTICE

Clearly, hands-on practice using the electronic resource is the preferred method of providing information to workshop participants. Combined with an opening demonstration, hands-on practice best fits the principles of adult learning.

Here are some things to keep in mind when developing hands-on workshop sessions.

- Subject specific, practical hands-on examples are best. If you can, have the participants come to the workshop with real examples from their work.
- Difficult tasks should be broken down into individual parts that can be practiced separately.
- Hands-on examples should be simple and short enough that the trainer can easily assist the participants. Trainers should know the answers in advance.
- If possible, have a floating helper in the back of the room who can assist participants who are having difficulty with the material.
- If the hands-on examples are from a national network, make sure the trainer checks the example immediately prior to the workshop.
- Feedback to learner should be immediate and precise.
- Let them play.

Frequently, equipment limits the number of people who can attend any given session. The buddy system of pairing two people per terminal or PC is often used in these situations. While the disadvantage of each participant getting less real time on the equipment is an issue, the advantage of participants teaching each other can significantly increase the rate of learning.

Did you know: Different adults learn in different ways. Planning a workshop that uses only one style, e.g., lecture, will not be as effective as a combination of different approaches. Whenever possible combine a lecture with handouts, a demonstration with hands-on, etc.

Keep in mind the participants' need for comfort, variety, recreation, and both social and solitary time.

OTHER FORMATS

There is a wide variety of other formats that can be used in workshops, including case studies, role playing, facilitated discussions, field trips, simulations, brainstorming, and fish bowl exercises. The list is nearly endless. While these other formats are not as directly applicable to teaching electronic resources, there are times when they may fit the agenda perfectly. For example, a field trip to a library that is successfully using the electronic resource under discussion can provide realistic information as well as break up a long day. In this example of a Telnet workshop, a facilitated discussion on how to use the Telnet command to support interlibrary loan and resource sharing could be the perfect capstone to the event. Remember that adults like variety and if you can find innovative ways of using the more participatory workshop formats, the better your workshop will be.

BREAKOUT GROUPS AND TRACKS

Another excellent way to add variety to a workshop is to use either break-out groups or tracks. These techniques work best when you have a significant number of participants, e.g., 40 or more. Breaking large groups into smaller groups can bring immediacy to the session. It also encourages more direct participation from attendees. Tracks are arranged around specific topics. Having several different tracks allows participants to self-select the topics of most immediate concern to their needs. For example, this Telnet workshop example could be expanded to have one track dedicated to Telnet resources and another to using Gophers.

BLOCKING OUT THE PROGRAM

THE OPENING SESSION

The opening session is critical to the workshop success. If you will recall, the Law of Primacy suggests that participants will remember the first and last part of the workshop best. So put lots of punch into the start. Most of all, set your tone—be enthusiastic!

Participants want to be assured that they'll get what they came for in the workshop. Communicate the agenda before the event. Place the agenda in the conference packet and display it in prominent places in the facility.

Keep your introductions, greetings, and thank yous brief. Break them up throughout the workshop if you have a lot of material to present. But don't forget to explain the facility to the attendees, especially restrooms and break areas. Start your sessions on time, especially the opening sessions because this will build in the expectation that the agenda will be followed.

Opening sessions can be used to build the necessary background information for the rest of the workshop. Here a renowned keynote speaker can draw attendance to your workshop and set the tone for the entire event.

PLANNING THE DAY

How long should each session last? Each session will have its own dynamic. A few simple principles can help you decide how to block out your workshop.

- Remember, adults like variety.
- Build in lots of free time and play time.
- Allow time for people to become acquainted.
- Coffee breaks should last at least 20 minutes if not longer.
- Never cancel or cut into breaks.
- The more variety inside the session, the longer the session can be and still hold interest.
- Intersperse complex topics with lighter ones.
- Don't have a session that goes longer than two hours without a break in the middle.
- Provide optional activities during free time, such as exhibits, access to computers, etc.
- Plan social events in the evening.

> Adults have shorter listening and viewing spans of attention than participating spans of attention.
> Reserve longer time slots for discussions, project work, and hands-on sessions.

THE CLOSING SESSION

Participants will want a chance to reflect and talk about unresolved issues. This is a good time to build in discussion sessions that focus on consensus building. The opportunity to evaluate the session should be encouraged at the closing session. Give participants a chance to bring closure and say good-bye.

CONSIDER THE COSTS

Developing a workshop budget is important. It will ensure your sponsoring agency that any up front cost will be returned. It will also help keep the workshop within reasonable bounds. The budget should include consideration of the following costs:

1. Communications: stationery, postage, duplication, and phone calls
2. Facility: rents, transportation, food, and lodging
3. Activities: program costs, equipment rentals, handouts, speaker fees, and accommodations
4. Special materials: films, computer programs, network connections, graphic materials, and first-aid kit
5. Registration materials: information packet, pencils, paper, and name tags
6. Contingency

Local businesses or electronic resources vendors may be interested in contributing to the costs of the workshop for the price of including their advertising somewhere in the program. Watch for ways of keeping the costs low for the participants. Most conference attendees appreciate learning about the companies that sell these services.

REGISTRATION

A registration form has two functions. It provides detailed information about the workshop to the potential participants as well as information about the participants to the workshop planners. The following information should be included in the registration form:

- Goals and objectives of the workshop
- The program in as much detail as possible, including speakers
- Dates, including opening and closing times
- Place, including accommodations
- Registration information, including fee, early registration fee, availability of on-site registration, limits on registration including cut-off date
- Refund policy
- List of materials to bring to the workshop

Once pre-registration forms start coming in, set up a ledger to record each participant's name, check number, and date-in. You'll want to bring this ledger to the registration table. Send pre-registrants a receipt along with a map and parking information. If any of the training materials or handouts can be sent early, include them. Some participants will want to come prepared for the sessions.

You will need to have an on-site registration table even if you aren't allowing on-site registration. There will always be some confusion about registration, and attendees need a visible place to sort out problems and ask questions. A visible banner should be placed above the registration table. The registration table should include a sign-in sheet and provide name tags.

Conference packets can also be distributed at the time of registration. These packets may include lists of participants including their E-mail addresses, a map of the facility, a workshop agenda with room numbers, training materials and handouts, paper, pencils, etc.—whatever you determine will aid the workshop participants. You may be able to recoup the cost of the conference packet by adding advertising.

Basic Network Survival Course:

**A library-oriented workshop on
regional, national, and international networks**

Sponsored by NMLA's Online Round Table

WHEN: **February 5, 1996, 9 a.m. to 5 p.m.**
WHERE: **New Mexico State University's New Library, Las Cruces**
COST: **$10 NMLA members, $12 non-members**

Cost includes lunch, refreshment breaks, and a packet of network information including "Internet Accessible Library Catalogs and Databases" and "Zen and the Art of the Internet."

— Schedule —

9–10 a.m.	Registration and tours of New Library	
10–10:20 a.m.	Overview of the nets	V. Horton, NMSU Library
10:20–10:45 a.m.	Equipment/connection needs to access the Net	J. Harris, NMSU C.C.
10:45 a.m.–noon	Regional networks (Technet, Zianet)	S. Rollins, UNM Library
Noon–1:15 p.m.	Lunch	
1:15–2:30 p.m.	National and international nets	A. St. George, UNM
2:30–2:45 p.m.	Break	
2:45–3:45 p.m.	FTP, Gopher, WAIS, BBS	S. Schilling, NMSU Library
3:45–5 p.m.	Hands-on the nets	

- -

Network Survival Course Registration

Name: _____ Phone: _____

Library: _____

Address: _____

I will be having lunch: no _____ yes _____ If yes, sandwich _____ or chef's salad _____

I will need local hotel information: no _____ yes _____

E-mail address: _____

Please make check payable to NMLA. Members: $10, Non-members: $12
Send to: Valerie Horton, NMSU Library, Box 30006, Dept. 3475, Las Cruces, NM 88003
Please return registration form by January 22, 1996; no in-house registration.
Previous experience with electronic mail will be helpful.

PUBLICITY

Publicizing the conference is a place for creativity and nerve! Depending on your audience, you may want to try a number of different venues for advertising your workshop. Don't forget word of mouth publicity, as it can be your most effective draw.

One of the most common forms of publicity is a paper flyer. This works well in sending to a discrete audience, i.e., teachers in a school, or mailing to a broader audience, i.e., all the librarians who are members of the state's library association. The flyers should have lots of sizzle. Find a volunteer who is artistically inclined or experienced with graphic design and desktop publishing. There is a large number of both inexpensive and/or sophisticated computer programs with graphics available to help you prepare a flashy flyer.

The flyer should include:

- The workshop goal and, if space, the objectives
- Program highlights and teasers
- Date, place, and time
- Registration fees
- Contact person for more information

The flyer should be brief and interesting. Sending it out with the registration form will provide participants with detailed information about the workshop.

There are a number of different methods for distributing your flyer, e.g., newsletters, targeted mailings, and bulletin boards. These days information can be distributed electronically. Many librarians have E-mail accounts or read Listservs, Usenet newsgroups, or other electronic bulletin boards. Many electronic literacy workshops appear over the Internet.

LIBRARIES ON THE

ELECTRONIC   FRONTIER

August 12, 1994
8:30 a.m. - 3.30 p.m.
(lunch not included)
New Library Classroom

Learn more about local and
global electronic information resources related to
your job and your personal information needs.

- **Telnet**
- **FTP/Archie**
- **Gopher**
- **DARNET**
- **Listserv**
- **Usenet New**

Brought to you by the Electronic Collections Task Force
& the Staff Training Committee, NMSU Library

SESSION MANAGEMENT

Electronic literacy programs require that background be provided on the resource under discussion. Make sure each session dealing with a new electronic resource includes:

- Descriptions of the product or database
- Product or database coverage
- Information on constructing searches
- Demonstrated examples
- Where to find print and online help
- A chance to use the resource

> No matter how short the program time is, always allow participants a chance to ask questions or make comments.

Again, equipment for the programs is vital in presenting electronic resources. Send each program presenter a form listing equipment needs. Include low-tech resources such as overhead projectors, facilitation tools such as flip charts or marker boards, audio-visual materials such as slide shows or sound systems, and high-tech tools such as presentation software. Presentation software has become very sophisticated. Presenters can create a wide range of graphics and special effects from programs such as Microsoft's Powerpoint or Harvard Graphics. Many of these presentation programs will print out copies of the slides which participants can use for note taking and later reference.

Workshop participants want "take away" handouts. Have presenters create instruction sheets for the user with enough information to get them started understanding basic themes. Handouts allow you to include additional advanced materials that may be beyond the scope or time frame of the session, but allows users to do self-directed learning. It is not a bad idea to color code handouts so users can keep track of the paper during and after the session.

According to the Principle of Exercise, the more an act is repeated the more quickly it is learned. Allow play time during the workshop during which users can get at equipment to practice what they learned in the sessions. Take home exercises with step-by-step practice sheets provide the participant with a method of practicing new skills after the workshop is over.

Sample Take-Home Handout

Internet Exercises
Telnetting to Remote Databases

Telnet is the Internet protocol for remote terminal connection service. It allows a user at one site to interact with a remote timesharing system at another site as if the user's terminal were connected directly to the remote computer.

Sample Exercise:

NMSU Library Catalog

What you type:	What it means:
1. Telnet library.nmsu.edu <Enter>	[establish connection with remote server]

Once you are logged onto a remote database, you'll need to learn how to use it. If you are familiar with the system you log into, feel free to start searching. If not, look for a help command to get started. Type h, help, or ? if nothing else works.

2. 1 <Enter>	[select database to search]
3. / ? <Enter>	[access system's help screen]
4. <Enter>	[exit help]
5. /quit <Enter>	[exit system]

- -

Your Turn...

The following are some exercises for you to try.

I. Law/Judicial Information and Catalogs

What you type:	What it means:
1. Telnet sparc-1.law.columbia.edu	[establish connection with remote server]
2. lawnet <Enter>	[logon to remote server]
3. <Enter>	[confirm terminal emulation]
4. q <Enter>	[exit the system]
5. q <Enter>	[confirm exit]

II. Library of Congress Catalog

What you type:	What it means:
1. Telnet locis.loc.gov <Enter>	[establish connection with remote server]
2. 7 <Enter>	[access system's help screen]
3. 12 <Enter>	[backup to main menu]
4. 12 <Enter>	[exit system]

For each program on the agenda, have a contingency plan. What if the presenter cancels? What if the equipment doesn't work? Have someone in mind who can step in and do a replacement program. Have transparencies for all electronic presentations available in case the equipment fails. Have back-up equipment available. Pre-planning at this stage can save you considerable trouble later.

ON-SITE ARRANGEMENTS

One person should be designated as the on-site facilitator or arranger. This person should have full responsibility to handle any circumstances that arise. An outline of the program with clearly marked descriptions of what is needed at each point in the program should be available to anyone helping with arrangements. Have a meeting before registration opens to make sure all your volunteers know their tasks.

On the day of the conference have extras of everything on hand, e.g., extra registration packets, extra food and drinks, blank name tags, extra equipment, etc. Make sure signs and maps are available as well as the equipment necessary to make impromptu signs. The following is a list of what to bring with you on the day of the workshop.

- Easel and newsprint pads
- Assorted color markers
- Scotch tape, masking tape, electrical tape
- Thumb tacks
- Banners
- Name tags for late registrants
- Extra agendas with room assignment
- Plastic cups, paper towels, napkins, plates, forks, and spoons
- Coffee creamers, assorted teas, sugar, etc.
- Spare light bulbs (especially for overhead projectors)
- Extension cords
- 3-prong adapters
- Serial and parallel cables
- First-aid kit
- Phone number and addresses of emergency services

Here is a final note about on-site arrangements. Be prepared for things to go wrong by planning for alternatives. Also, prepare yourself mentally; something will go wrong that wasn't in your contingency plans. Expect it, accept it, and be creative and flexible in handling it. Remember to laugh about it later!

EVALUATIONS

Workshop evaluations often get more lip-service than action. There are good reasons to evaluate your workshop. These include:

- Determining how well your program met its objectives
- Making decisions related to program improvement or future workshop planning
- Providing feedback to program presenters
- Showing accountability
- Providing a learning experience for program planners

Don't slight your evaluation. Think of it as your chance to learn. Evaluation criteria should be directly related to the objectives. There are numerous ways of doing evaluations. Evaluation forms are one of the most common methods. A sample evaluation form is shown on the next page, but there are numerous other styles that may be used. Choose the style that fits your workshop.

BASIC NETWORK SURVIVAL COURSE
EVALUATION

1. Prior to this workshop, how would you rate your network experience?

   Experienced   Novice

     5   4   3   2   1

2. How would you rate the following items?
   (3 for Excellent, 2 for Good, 1 for Poor—you can repeat numbers)

   Programs: _____

   Hands-on computer time: _____

   Conference packet: _____

   Practice exercises: _____

   Short guides to retrieving network resources   _____

3. How would you rate the sessions?
   (3 for Excellent, 2 for Good, 1 for Poor—you can repeat numbers)

   Overview of the nets: _____

   Connections to the nets: _____

   Regional networks: _____

   Internet universe: _____

   Hands-on demonstrations: _____

4. How would you rate the workshop overall:

   Excellent   Poor

     5   4   3   2   1

5. Would you be interested in attending an advanced Internet workshop?

   Yes: _____   No: _____

6. General comments (use back if necessary):

Another type of evaluation technique is the focus groups. Traditionally, focus groups are in-person groups of six or seven participants run by a trained facilitator. A new type of electronic focus group is emerging across the networks. You can form an electronic discussion group where you can post questions and allow a discussion to ensue among those participants who have E-mail accounts. The free flowing nature of electronic discussions can provide planners with an overwhelming amount of often conflicting information, but all of it is valuable in learning how to prepare for your next electronic literacy workshop.

FOLLOW–UP

Participants who leave an electronic literacy workshop often feel overwhelmed. They want to know where to begin and where to go for help. There are things you can do to meet this need. As discussed earlier, have handouts with both instructions and take home exercises available. Electronic discussion groups can be used not only for evaluation, but also to allow participants to ask questions and get help. Have your presenters give their E-mail addresses out during their sessions. Encourage your learners to contact these experts. There are thousands of Listservs and Usenet newgroups dedicated to almost every electronic literacy topic. Inform participants how to sign up for related electronic discussion groups.

Follow-up also includes closing down the details of the workshop. There will be bills to pay, cost sheets to submit, and reports to sponsoring agencies to write. Make sure you send thank yous to speakers and volunteers.

APPENDIX A:
WORKSHOP PLANNING TIMETABLE

6 months prior to the event	Identify possible presenters
	Identify possible facilities
	Obtain volunteer helpers
	Select date and times
5 months prior to the event	Visit facilities and secure location
	Arrange for meals and lodging if applicable
	Decide on how equipment will be handled
	Obtain commitments from presenters
4 months prior to the event	Identify publicity opportunities
	Develop publicity flyers, press releases, etc.
	Develop pre-registration materials
3 months prior to the event	Start publicizing the workshop
	Survey presenters' equipment needs
	Arrange for presenters' travel requirements
1 month before the event	Confirm all arrangements
2 weeks before the event	Assemble conference packets
Immediately prior to the event	Complete registration table materials
	Confirm presenter requirements
	Check equipment set-up
Day of the event	Be there early and stay to keep an eye on everything
	Set up registration table
	Orient volunteer helpers
After the event	Send thank-you letters
	Process bills and reimbursements
	Tabulate evaluations and distribute results
	Report to sponsoring agency

REFERENCE

1. *Treasury of Techniques for Teaching Adults* (National Association for Public School Adult Education, 1964), p. 2.

CREATING AN ELECTRONIC INFORMATION LITERACY COURSE

Keith Gresham
University of Colorado at Boulder Library

The author wishes to acknowledge John Culshaw and Ben LoBue, reference librarians at the University of Colorado at Boulder, for the initial design of several of the course materials reproduced in this chapter.

A variety of instructional methods is used by librarians to help prepare college students for an information-based society, including course-related and course-integrated instruction, workshops, seminars, individualized instruction, and printed and electronic tutorials. A less common but potentially effective option is the creation of a formal credit course in electronic information literacy. When developed and delivered using a concept-based approach appropriate to student needs, a credit course provides an in-depth exploration of electronic technology that teaches students the information-seeking strategies, critical thinking abilities, and life-long learning skills needed in an information society.[1]

This chapter will examine the strengths and weaknesses of the credit course model of instruction, provide a brief discussion of concept-based instruction, and describe the basic organizational and instructional design decisions required in creating a formal course. It will also provide sample course goals and objectives, a course description and syllabus, and assignments for an electronic information literacy course.

CREDIT COURSE AS INSTRUCTIONAL MODEL

As the basic instructional unit found in higher education, the credit course concept is not unknown to academic librarians. In the credit course model, students formally register for a given academic course with the understanding that their successful participation in course activities and assignments will result in academic credit earned toward a degree. What may be less clear to many librarians, however, is how to develop a formal quarter- or semester-long course and how such a course differs from other instructional programs in the library.

Instructional programs found in most academic libraries today follow the course-related instructional model.[2] In the course-related model, the librarian usually functions as the "guest instructor" for one or two sessions of a course offered by a specific subject department. In such instruction, both the depth of lesson content and the amount of time for active learning activities are usually limited. In the credit course model, however, the librarian (or team of librarians) is responsible for designing and teaching the entire course and can devote as much time to a particular topic or activity as needed. Course concepts can be introduced and sequenced at an appropriate pace so as to encompass the full range of electronic resources available to student researchers. As with any teaching model, the credit course carries both advantages and disadvantages:[3]

ADVANTAGES

- Flexible format allows instructors to experiment with a wide variety of course activities.
- Multiple class sessions and a variety of activities accommodate differing student learning styles.
- Length of course allows for in-depth exploration of course concepts.
- Weekly sessions promote a high level of student/instructor interaction.
- Student readiness and motivation can be relatively high.
- Numerous design models are available in the professional literature.

DISADVANTAGES

- Course design, class preparation, and delivery of instruction require a heavy time commitment.
- Detailed scope of the course requires some level of teaching expertise.
- Facilities, equipment, and costs place limits on the number of students reached.
- Certain aspects of course structure are dictated by institutional policies.

Clearly, in spite of its limitations, a formal information literacy course is not meant to replace other instruction programs in the library. Certain students will always have the need for orientation, a workshop or course-related instruction, or point-of-use guides. Each of these techniques succeeds in its own way and should not be readily discarded. Similiarly, certain other students will also strongly benefit from a systematic long-term examination of information-seeking concepts and strategies—an educational experience unique to the credit course model. The proper use of an information literacy course, therefore, is as an additional component in an already diverse set of instructional programs offered by the college library.

GATHERING INFORMATION

Conducting some level of a needs assessment is a crucial preliminary step in developing a credit course. You must have some idea of the perceived and actual instructional needs of your target audience before you can decide what goals or objectives your course should accomplish. Gathering information for a needs assessment can involve a variety of methods and instruments.[4] The following methods, either individually or in combination, can reveal unexpected answers concerning students' perception of the role of the library and of library research in their lives.

- Focus groups
- Interviews
- User surveys or questionnaires
- Pre-tests and post-tests
- Analysis of library mission and goals
- Inventory of electronic library resources
- Library resource use patterns

Figure 1 [all figures appear at the end of this chapter] reproduces part of a sample needs assessment survey aimed at undergraduate students. Because the library research needs of students are usually tied to their coursework in other classes, you might also want to gather information from appropriate subject department faculty on campus.

In addition to a needs assessment, a careful examination of both campus and library organizational structures is helpful in providing a profile of the environment where the credit course will exist. Each of following areas should be examined:[5]

- Institutional goals
- Institutional political structure
- Library mission and goals
- Existing instructional programs and services
- Budget and staffing patterns
- Available technologies
- Evaluation methods

Once information has been collected, analyze the results. Identify all the student needs that emerge. Determine how, or even if, a credit course can realistically meet any or all of the student expectations. Observable patterns and trends will help you decide which needs can best be met by a credit course and which can best be achieved through other instructional programs. Once specific student needs have been identified, analyzed, and linked to the library's educational mission, you will be well prepared to build the necessary support for the creation of the course.

SEEKING SUPPORT

Instructional programs do not exist in a vacuum and are not created through the efforts of a single librarian. As a library service offered in support of the educational mission of the campus, a credit course requires the support and commitment of the library administration to succeed. And, because library resources—including time and money—will be spent developing and delivering the course, it is important that all departments in the library understand how a credit course fits within the library's educational mission. A strategically written proposal supported by the information gathered in the needs assessment will help administrators and colleagues develop that understanding.

The process for gaining approval for a credit course depends upon the political structure of your campus. If your library is a faculty department, approval by the library dean and appropriate library faculty committee is likely to be required. On some campuses, approval from a curriculum committee outside the library might also be required.

If your library is not a faculty department, you may have to ask another department on campus to sponsor your course. Academic libraries have successfully integrated their credit courses into general studies, library science, humanities, English composition, and honors departments. Similar or other options may exist on your campus.

BUILDING THE FOUNDATION

Once support and approval for the course have been won, you will need to make some practical decisions regarding the underlying structure of the course.[6] Because these seemingly random choices will later affect all aspects of course design, your foundational decisions should be based on more than just personal preference. To guide you in these early decisions, again examine the educational mission of your institution, the educational and curricular needs of your students, and the existing instructional programs and resources within your library.

REQUIRED OR ELECTIVE COURSE

The course design offered in this chapter follows an elective course model. While some institutions have developed and implemented required library skills courses, recent surveys suggest that many academic libraries have abandoned campus-wide required library courses in favor of smaller, more specialized elective courses.[7] This refocusing of resources can be attributed to an increased awareness of current learning theory and the economic downsizing faced by most libraries today.

Current learning theory suggests that an information literacy course must reach students at appropriate times in their academic careers, when information concepts and processes can be immediately applied to ongoing coursework in other classes.[8] The appropriate times, however, differ among individual students. This is why a stand-alone required course, i.e., a required course not contextually integrated into an individual degree program, rarely succeeds. The course exists in an artificial context, tends to view all students as the same, and rarely reaches the intended audience at the right time or place.

A stand-alone credit course set up as an elective, however, is inherently responsive to individualized student needs. An elective course gives students the option of taking the course at an appropriate time in their program of study and, therefore, tends to attract self-motivated students who already see, on some level, the practical application of course content to their needs.

Economic realities must also be addressed. As library budgets continue to shrink, few libraries have the necessary personnel or resources to sustain a required, campus-wide course. Enrollment in an elective course, however, is easily controlled and can be increased or scaled back as resources allow.

COURSE LEVEL

While an electronic information literacy course can be designed for any student level, choosing a specific level to target early on is critical to the course's success. A course will not succeed if it ignores the differing instructional needs of a sophomore working on a five-page essay and a graduating senior working on a honors thesis. Some libraries offer lower-division courses so that they may teach introductory information literacy concepts to students early in their academic lives. Other libraries create upper-division courses for those students who are beginning work on major research projects or senior theses. Still others design graduate level courses for students who are in the early stages of thesis or dissertation research. While no one approach is better than the other, the choice of a target audience is important because it determines the specific concepts and resources you will later incorporate into class activities and assignments.

The following questions may help you decide which level of student would most likely benefit from the type of course you wish to design:

- Which students have an immediate need for the types of concepts taught in the course?
- Which students would most likely find an immediate application for the concepts?
- What level of students is not already being served by existing course-integrated or course-related library sessions?
- What level of research does the library's electronic resources support?
- What level of courses from other departments would the information literacy course best serve?

CREDIT HOURS

An electronic information literacy course can offer any number of credit hours depending on how you structure the course. In most campus departments, the number of credit hours offered for a course is determined by a combination of factors, including course level, the number of hours the class meets each week, and student workload requirements. Typically, the more rigorous or time-consuming the course, the higher the number of credit hours offered. With the exception of remedial skills classes, most credit courses taught by libraries offer between two and three credit hours. Curriculum committees and departmental offices at your institution can provide you with appropriate guidelines.

NUMBER OF SECTIONS

The number of course sections you offer depends primarily upon the number of librarians involved in teaching the class and student demand for the course. If you are the only instructor for the course, one or two sections will probably be all that your schedule allows. If your institution has a team of librarians who share teaching duties, then more sections might be possible. Obviously, the more sections you offer, the more students you can reach each academic term. However, because it takes time for a newly created elective course to find an audience, initial student demand may not warrant more than one section per term. A sensible approach is to start small and expand the number of course sections as time and resources allow.

MEETING CONFIGURATION

Depending upon your campus scheduling policies, you may have some flexibility in how you arrange the meeting hours of your class. Generally, longer blocks of time are preferable with courses that make use of active-learning techniques and hands-on practice. In a two-credit course, for example, you might want to consider meeting for a single two-hour session each week rather than two one-hour sessions.

ENROLLMENT LIMIT

Unlike a straight lecture course that can accommodate as many students as can fit in a given classroom, a course that stresses the practical uses of electronic resources is unlikely to work with large numbers of students. Even if your campus computing labs or electronic classrooms can accommodate large groups, you will probably find that offering active-learning techniques, small group activities, and hands-on exercises in the course is difficult once your class size exceeds 28 to 30 students.

GRADED OR PASS-FAIL

The grading policies and registration procedures on your campus might allow you to choose whether you want to offer a graded course or a pass-fail course. While student motivation tends to be higher in a graded course, some students might legitimately benefit from a pass-fail grading system. The best solution, if available, is to offer the course with both options and let the student decide which option best meets her or his own individual needs.

MEETING SPACE

In choosing a suitable meeting space, it helps to think about the kind of activities you wish to incorporate into the class sessions. For example, hands-on activities require access to computers; online or CD-ROM search strategy demonstrations are typically more effective if the computer screen is projected in front of the classroom; and small group learning techniques usually benefit from clusters of tables rather than rows of desks. Once you have some idea of the type of instructional activities you will be using, investigate the various electronic classroom options available on your campus. An ideal meeting space would be a room within the library that provides clusters of tables for small-group work, a central computer with CD-ROM drive connected to an LCD panel display that projects the computer screen up in front of the class, and a separate cluster of networked computers that allows students to practice searching techniques using CD-ROM databases, online systems, or Internet sources. Such an all-purpose electronic classroom is not the only option, however. Often a combination of meeting spaces—including traditional classrooms, library labs, electronic classrooms, and campus computing labs—can be used throughout the course, depending on the particular needs of an individual class session.

DESIGNING THE COURSE

CONCEPT-BASED INSTRUCTION

Concept-based library instruction refers to a teaching approach that emphasizes processes and general principles of research that can be taught and transferred from one research situation to another. Such instruction focuses on teaching problem-solving strategies students can use with a wide variety of electronic sources.[9] Thus, a concept-based course responds to the long-term information needs of students.

An opposite approach, tool-based instruction, focuses on the distinctive features or procedural aspects of operating individual databases. However, because technologies change over time and vary from one library to another, a course focused primarily on specific tools will not provide students with the conceptual understanding needed later to integrate unfamiliar or newer electronic sources into an information search.[10]

A concept-based approach, although focused on the research process, does not ignore the various types of electronic sources available to researchers. The sources and their corresponding operating concepts, i.e., Boolean operators, field searching, controlled vocabulary, network connections, etc., are introduced and taught to students within the context of the research process, and integrated into the course at appropriate times and places.

COURSE GOAL AND OBJECTIVES

Goals and objectives are essential components of the creation process. Goals describe the major purpose or aim of the course, and objectives describe the specific concrete steps toward achieving the goals. Initially, both will assist you in developing an overall organizational structure for the course and will allow you to identify and choose appropriate course topics. Later on, goals and objectives also provide you with one means of evaluating the course.

The form, structure, and intent of course goals and objectives can vary. In the cognitive tradition of learning theory, objectives (sometimes referred to as terminal objectives) focus on the specific course concepts or research processes to be taught and the ways in which these concepts and processes are related to one another:[11]

> students understand how specific bibliographic elements of information sources are organized in electronic systems and how these elements influence access and retrieval.

In the behavioralist tradition of learning theory, objectives (sometimes referred to as enabling objectives) focus less on the processes of research and more on the measurable or observable actions or behaviors required of students to achieve the terminal objectives:[12]

> students will identify important bibliographic data by correctly organizing a bibliographic citation according to a given style manual.

Although examples of enabling objectives are widely available in the literature, model terminal objectives are more difficult to locate. In 1987, the Bibliographic Instruction Section of the Association of College and Research Libraries developed a model set of terminal objectives well suited for use in an electronic information literacy course.[13] Sample course objectives based on this model are shown in Figure 2.

COURSE TOPICS AND CONCEPTUAL FRAMEWORK

Course topics should relate to identified student needs, the corresponding course goals and objectives you have developed, and the specific electronic information resources found in your library. How these topics are arranged, sequenced, and introduced in the course depend upon the organizational structure or conceptual framework you select.

Although many conceptual frameworks for library instruction have been identified, one that works particularly well in an electronic information literacy course is a modified version of the framework known as systematic literature searching.[14] This model is built upon the idea that library research is a systematic process that requires a researcher to analyze the nature and character of the research question, focus on the specific information need, choose appropriate access resources, and construct a search strategy to identify, locate, and evaluate relevant information.

One of the strengths of this model is that a concept-based strategy for information searching can be taught in combination with a hands-on exploration of the types of information sources and their electronic access tools. The electronic resources are placed within their proper context in the search process.

Using a systematic literature searching framework, an electronic information literacy course could focus on the following topics:

- Creation and transmission of information (both popular and scholarly communication).
- Structures of information (subject classification, subject headings, database record structure, etc.).
- Physical arrangement of information (academic subject areas, subject-specific collections, etc.).
- Construction, application, and revision of a search strategy.
- Access to information (reference sources, periodical indexes, Gopher sites, etc.).
- Electronic searching concepts (Boolean searching, field searching, controlled vocabulary, etc.).
- Uses and structures of information among different academic disciplines.
- Evaluation of information.

In demonstrating and applying these concepts, a variety of electronic sources can be used:

- Online library catalog
- Periodical indexes on CD-ROM

- Full-text databases on CD-ROM
- Periodical indexes and full-text databases available online
- Internet resources

Numerous variations of this organizational framework are possible. Constructing an appropriate framework based on identified student needs, goals, and objectives will allow you to select and organize course content in a meaningful, systematic way.

COURSE SYLLABUS

The course syllabus, or class outline, is the manifestation of the organizational framework of the course. A syllabus provides a session-by-session description of topics to be covered throughout the course along with basic course and instructor information. The syllabus also serves as a "contract" between instructor and students in that it provides information about course content, assignments, grading procedures, and instructor expectations of students.

Creating the syllabus requires you first to examine the campus academic calendar, making note of the first and last class day, campus holidays, and the exam schedule. Once you know exactly how many class sessions you have to work with in the academic term, you are able to decide exactly when, in what order, and for how many sessions the individual course topics will be taught. A logical progression of course topics should be constructed, and assignments, examinations, and projects should be scheduled at appropriate times and places in the syllabus.

Information contained in a syllabus typically includes:

- Course name
- Meeting days, time, and place
- Instructor name, telephone, E-mail address, office location, and office hours
- Course requirements, assignments, and tests
- Day-by-day summary of course topics
- Assignment, test, and project due dates
- Grading procedures
- Required textbook or supplementary readings

A sample course syllabus is shown in Figure 3. Combined with the course goals and objectives, the syllabus provides a detailed overview of the entire course.

COURSE DESCRIPTION

A concise summary of your course will probably be needed for the course catalog or curricula bulletin. In addition to serving as a marketing tool to attract students, the official course description informs campus administrators, subject department faculty, and campus advisers of the official existence of the course. The course summary also allows other institutions to assess the academic content and intellectual rigor of the course when evaluating transcripts of transfer students.

In only a few paragraphs, a well-written course description can effectively express the guiding philosophy behind the creation of the course, provide a sense of the conceptual framework upon which the course is built, convey the basic content and focus of the course, and provide a sense of the practical applications of course content. A sample course description is shown in Figure 4.

COURSE ASSIGNMENTS AND TESTS

Assignments and tests, as performance measures, serve multiple functions in a formal course.[15] They provide students with practical opportunities to apply course topics and concepts through real and simulated research experiences using electronic resources. They also serve as a method of evaluating the progress of students in relation to stated course objectives. And, assignments and tests provide a relatively objective way of assigning student grades in the course.

Assignments should be developed in such a way as to reflect the major goals and objectives of the course, and, as with the course structure, should focus on the process of information research. The true value of an assignment is usually not in a student's answer, but rather in the process the student went through to arrive at an answer. Thus, process-oriented assignments work best when the relevancy of the assignment is readily apparent and linked to student interests and needs.

To increase their reliability as performance measures, assignments and tests should also be designed to reflect a wide variety of student learning styles. This can be achieved by varying the type and format of course activities:

- Process-based individual exercises
- Small group presentations
- Active-learning activities
- Workshop participation
- Research projects
- Process-based exam questions

Figures 5 through 11 provide examples of the various options available when designing assignments and test questions for an electronic information literacy course.

COURSE EVALUATION

Course evaluation is an ongoing process that occurs both informally and formally. Informal feedback is obtained by course instructors during the course through student comments and questions during class, through feedback from students after class or during office hours, and through student performance on class assignments and tests. Informal feedback allows the instructor to modify various aspects of the course during the academic term in response to student interests and needs.

Most institutions also offer a formal course evaluation survey that allows students to evaluate course content, organization, and instructor performance at the end of the academic term. Typically instructors can modify or add evaluation questions to the survey to increase the relevancy and specificity of student feedback. In addition to providing instructors with student feedback, formal course questionnaires are often used in the annual evaluation, reappointment, and tenure processes for librarians.

Information obtained through both formal and informal means allows you to review the course organization, revise course content and topics, make changes to the syllabus, and modify lessons or activities when appropriate. Ultimately, evaluation information should also be used continually to revisit your original needs assessment and reassess the course goals and objectives you developed. An ongoing process of review and revision is necessary to the course's continued success and will provide you with valuable information when called upon to justify the existence of the course to campus and library administrators, subject department faculty, students, and other librarians.

Figure 1 Needs Assessment Survey

Undergraduate Library Use Survey

1a. In which College or School are you currently enrolled?

_____College of Architecture and Planning   _____College of Engineering and Applied Sciences
_____College of Arts and Sciences   _____School of Journalism and Mass Communication
_____College of Business Administration   _____College of Music
_____School of Education   _____Undecided

1b. If you answered College of Arts and Sciences in 1a, which one of the following academic areas best describes your degree program?

_____Fine Arts   _____Social Sciences   _____Other
_____Humanities   _____Sciences

2. Which one of the following choices best describes your status as an undergraduate?

_____Freshman   _____Junior   _____Other
_____Sophomore   _____Senior

3. How many years have you been enrolled at this institution?

_____0-1   _____1-2   _____2-3   _____3-4   _____4 or more

4. Have you used the University libraries during this academic year?   _____Yes   _____No

5. Why do you use the University libraries? (mark all that apply)

_____Study on own   _____Borrow library materials
_____Study with group   _____Use audiovisual materials
_____Work on course assignments   _____Photocopy
_____Conduct research for term paper   _____Socialize
_____Check out reserve readings   _____Relax/sleep
_____Read current magazines or newspapers   _____Other

6. Which of the following instructional services have you used in the University libraries?

_____Class instruction   _____Library tours
_____Database instruction   _____Term-paper research counseling
_____Expanded reference   _____Other

7a. Do you have an account on the campus computer network?   _____Yes   _____No

7b. If you answered Yes in 7a, which services do you use?

_____University libraries' catalog   _____Gopher servers
_____Other libraries' online catalogs   _____Newsgroups and/or Listservs
_____Campus information system   _____Other campus computing services
_____Electronic mail   _____Other

8. How would you describe your overall satisfaction level with the University libraries?

_____Very satisfied   _____Satisfied   _____Not satisfied

Figure 2 Course Objectives

Methods of Library Research
Course Objectives

At the completion of the course, students should:
- Understand that information sources in libraries are physically organized and grouped in specific ways, including by academic discipline, subject, author, publisher, or format type.
- Understand that library personnel include individuals with varying degrees and areas of subject expertise who may be helpful in accessing information.
- Understand that there is a variety of research tools, both printed and electronic, whose primary purpose is to identify other information sources.
- Understand that these research tools vary by discipline and in the way they are structured and accessed.
- Understand the importance of selecting the appropriate research tool in order to identify useful information sources.
- Understand how to construct a research approach or search strategy appropriate to a particular information need.

Figure 3 Course Syllabus

Methods of Library Research

Tues/Thur 11:00–12:15   Rm. E303, Norlin Library

Keith Gresham   Office Hours
Phone: 555-5555   Tues/Thur, 12:15–1 pm
E-mail: gresham@cubldr.colorado.edu   Room E176, Norlin

Syllabus

August 25	Introduction; course objectives; syllabus; assignments
August 30	University libraries overview; Norlin Library tour
September 1	Structures of information: subject classification, subject headings, and database records
September 6	CARL computer system: introduction and basic searching
September 8	CARL computer system: advanced searching techniques **(assignment)**
September 13	Reference materials: subject guides, handbooks, bibliographies, directories
September 15	Reference materials: subject encyclopedias and dictionaries, biographical sources
September 20	Periodicals: an examination of the research process
September 22	CD-ROM indexes: introduction
September 27	CD-ROM indexes: basic searching strategies
September 29	CD-ROM indexes: advanced searching strategies **(assignment)**
October 4	Work day for group presentations
October 6	**Group presentations:** CD-ROM indexes
October 11	**Group presentations:** CD-ROM indexes
October 13	**Group presentations:** CD-ROM indexes
October 18	**EXAM**

Figure 3 Continued

October 20	Online database systems: FirstSearch, LEXIS-NEXIS
October 25	Online database systems: FirstSearch, LEXIS-NEXIS **(assignment)**
October 27	Scientific and technological research
November 1	Government/statistical research **(assignment)**
November 3	Virtual library: introduction to the Internet
November 8	Virtual library: searching the Internet
November 10	Virtual library: searching the Internet
November 15	Workshop: evaluating sources of information **(assignment)**
November 17	Workshop: evaluating sources of information **(assignment)**
November 22	Map and cartographic information research
November 24	Thanksgiving Break
November 29	Special collections/rare books
December 1	Future research technologies
December 6	Wrap up/course evaluation
	Pathfinder/Guide to the Literature due

Grading

Assignments (including group presentation)	1/3
Mid-term exam	1/3
Pathfinder/Guide to the Literature	1/3

Figure 4 Course Description

Methods of Library Research
Course Description

This course is designed to provide students with an in-depth and practical exploration of the structure, organization, retrieval, and evaluation of information within a chosen academic discipline. The course focuses on the formulation of search strategy, including the selection and evaluation of reference tools and electronic information sources, the selection of relevant information from such sources, and techniques for recording and organizing that information. The selection and evaluation of reference and information sources require a knowledge of the various types of sources and an understanding of the functions and values of particular sources.

In addition to looking at representative examples from different categories of printed reference materials, this course includes in-depth instruction in the incorporation of electronic reference tools (including the library's online catalog, bibliographic and full-text electronic databases, and selected Internet resources) into the research process.

The assignments throughout the course do not require students simply to find and retrieve sources, but rather serve to encourage students to think critically while engaged in academic research.

Figure 5 Online System Assignment

CARL Online System

For each of the questions below, indicate the most appropriate CARL database to use, the most **efficient** search strategy you would use, and the search results or answer. If the question asks where the University libraries keeps a particular item, be sure to list both **call number and location.**

1. Who is the author of the *Witches of Eastwick*? If the University libraries owns this book, where is it kept?

    DATABASE:

    SEARCH STRATEGY:

    ANSWER:

2. I'm looking for a book for young children that deals with homelessness. I heard that an author named Sendak wrote a book on this subject and that the word "dumps" is supposed to be in the title. What's the full title of the book and where can I find it in the University libraries?

    DATABASE:

    SEARCH STRATEGY:

    ANSWER:

3. What is the title and who are the authors of the first article in Volume 58, Number 4, of the *American Sociological Review*?

    DATABASE:

    SEARCH STRATEGY:

    ANSWER:

4. The University libraries owns one copy of *Gender Shock* by Hester Eisenstein, but suppose the library catalog says that the book is checked out. What other four libraries in the region say they also own the book?

    DATABASE:

    SEARCH STRATEGY:

    ANSWER:

5. How many books do the University libraries own by an author named Bruce Bawer?

    DATABASE:

    SEARCH STRATEGY:

    ANSWER:

Figure 6 CD-ROM Index Assignment

Periodical Indexes on CD-ROM
Group Presentation

In order to locate specific journal, magazine, or newspaper articles on a given topic, a researcher must use a periodical index. Before the 1980s, most periodical indexes appeared in book/printed form. Every year, more and more periodical indexes are being produced in electronic form using CD-ROM technology. Most of these electronic periodical indexes are devoted to providing access (or more literally, a citation) to the periodical literature of a given subject or discipline.

In an effort to explore and learn about the wide variety of searching options on these various databases, we are devoting three class sessions to group demonstrations and presentations. Each group, composed of three individuals, is to choose one specific CD-ROM database to introduce and teach to the rest of the class. Group presentations should last a maximum of 15 minutes. A group may divide up its presentation in any way it chooses, but the demonstration should show that all individuals contributed equally.

Suggested outline and points to cover, include:

I. Introduction
   - Name of database
   - Subject content
   - Intended audience or user
   - Scope (journals, magazines, newspapers, or some combination)
   - Coverage (comprehensive, selective, etc.)
   - Dates of coverage
   - Frequency of issue (bimonthly, monthly, quarterly, less often)
   - Lag time (how long between the time the article is printed and the citation appears)
   - Method of indexing (subject, author, title, etc.)
   - Record structure (simple or complex; use of fields; contain abstracts?)
   - Any other info that you think the class should know to make use of the database?

II. Demonstration
   Demonstrate two or three search strategies for example research topics that make use of your database's searching capabilities. For some databases, you might need to touch upon the use of a thesaurus, controlled vocabulary, descriptors, Boolean operators/logical connectors, truncation, nesting, field searching, free-text searching, etc. Make sure your demos are clear and to the point . . . remember that you are trying to teach this database to people who may have never seen or used it before.

III. Questions from the Audience
   Groups should be able to answer any questions or clarify any points. Groups should also be prepared to devise a search strategy and conduct a search on a topic of the instructor's choosing.

Figure 7 Search Strategy Assignment

Electronic Database Search Strategies

Develop a search strategy for each of the following topics. Be sure to include the following steps in developing each strategy:

a) Select an appropriate database from the list.
b) Explain why you chose the database.
c) Could more than one database be used for the search? How would the results differ if you used another database?
d) Develop your strategy for the chosen database:—identify the search topic—separate the concepts—think of other words for the concepts (vocabulary)—consider variations in word endings (truncation)—connect the concepts (Boolean/logical operators).
e) Explain what kind of search results you would expect to see.

Use these databases in developing your search strategies:
- Sociofile
- Periodical Abstracts
- Newspaper Abstracts
- Social Sciences Index
- Humanities Index
- ERIC

1. Locate journal articles dealing with political and economic changes in Eastern Europe.

2. Find magazine or newspaper articles that address the portrayal of ethnic groups, i.e., Native Americans, African-Americans, Italians, etc., in film.

3. Locate articles that discuss competitive pressures in the sport of figure skating and how those pressures can lead to physical violence.

4. Search for scholarly articles on the effects of television on children.

5. Find a study that focuses on the moral or ethical questions (rather than the social implications) surrounding the issue of physician-assisted suicide.

Figure 8 Business Research Assignment

Business Research Using Electronic Databases

Select a major U.S. public corporation you would like to work for in the future. The company you choose should be the parent company and not a subsidiary of a larger corporation. It is also important that your company be publicly owned by shareholders.

COMPANY: _____

Look for information about your company in each of the following electronic databases. Keep in mind that some electronic databases serve as indexes, while others contain full-text documents.
 a) ABI/Inform
 b) Compact Disclosure
 c) General Business File
 d) NEXIS Business File
For each of the four databases, write a paragraph description about what type of information you are finding within that specific database. Within each paragraph, you may also want to address any of the following issues:
 •   Is the information contained within the database scholarly, popular, or in between?
 •   How is this database different from the other databases looked at in class?
 •   How does the searching capability of this database compare with other databases?
 •   What do the contents of this database tell you about the nature of business research?
 •   How might this database be used within the subject discipline you have chosen for your final project?

Figure 9 Internet Exploration Assignment

Internet Exploration Workshop

A) LOG-IN: Log into your campus computer account. If login was successful, the computer should respond with the name of your host computer.

B) E-MAIL:
 •   At your host computer prompt, type: **pine**
 •   Send your instructor an E-mail message to: **gresham@cubldr.colorado.edu**
 •   Add the E-mail address of one of your classmates to your electronic address book. Send that person a short E-mail message.

C) GOPHER: Part One
 •   At your host name prompt, type: **gopher gopher.lib.umich.edu**
 •   Follow the path: **What's New & Featured Resources** →
                                      Clearinghouse for Subject-Oriented Internet Resource Guides →
 •   Explore the following archives: **Guides on the Humanities/**
                                      Guides on the Sciences/
                                      Guides on the Social Sciences/
 •   Within the guides at this Gopher site, locate five potential Internet resources for your chosen final project topic. Mail any interesting resources back to you via your E-mail address. NOTE: **Proper citation format for a Gopher site consists of the Gopher address and the numeration/pathname(s) you followed to locate the information.**

Figure 10 Sample Exam Questions

Exam Questions

A. **The Library of Congress Subject Heading (LCSH) books provide you with the "vocabulary" to use when searching for books by subject. Using the LCSH books, answer the following questions. (6 points)**

   1) If I wanted to find a book on the subject of "environmental tourism," what are the search words I should use according to LCSH?

   2) Look up the subject phrase "drug abuse" in the LCSH. According to LCSH, what is a broader search term for this subject?

B. **A sample record from the ERIC database is reproduced below. Each field in the record is labeled with a two- or three-letter abbreviation that describes the type of citation information that is contained in that field.**

   AN: EJ449908
   CHN: EA527058
   AU: Molnar,-Alex
   TI: Too Many Kids Are Getting Killed.
   PY: 1992
   JN: Educational-Leadership; v50 n1 p4-5 Sep 1992
   SN: ISSN-0013-1784
   AV: UMI
   DT: Journal Articles (080); Reports - Evaluative (142)
   LA: English
   DE: Affluent-Youth; Elementary-Secondary-Education; Poverty-
   DE: *Child-Advocacy; *Educational-Practices; *Peace-; *School-Responsibility; *Violence-
   ID: *Peace-Education
   IS: CIJJAN93
   AB: For too many children, our society is a fearful wasteland that mocks adult pieties and nurtures nihilism. The threat of violence cannot be dispelled with metal detectors, weapons checks, and secured hallways. Educators must adopt classroom practices that promote and strengthen peaceful relations among students and become more effective advocates for children and their families. (MLH)

   For each of the following field abbreviations, briefly explain what type of information is being provided in that field. (6 points)
   AU:
   TI:
   PY:
   JN:
   LA:
   AB:

Figure 10 Continued

C. Reproduced below is a sample page from the Thesaurus of Sociological Indexing Terms, the thesaurus used when searching the Sociofile database.

Domestic Science
    Use Home Economics

Domestic Servants
    Use Domestics

Domestic Violence
    Use Family Violence

Downs Syndrome
    UF Mongoloidism
    RT Congenitally Handicapped
         Genetics
         Handicapped
         Mentally Retarded

Dowry
    RT Bridewealth
         Marriage

Family Violence
    UF Conjugal Violence
         Domestic Violence
    BT Violence
    NT Child Abuse
         Spouse Abuse
    RT Abuse
         Assault
         Battered Women
         Child Neglect
         Elder Abuse
         Family

Using the sample page, answer the following three questions. (12 points)

1) If I'm searching Sociofile for citations to articles that talk about the causes of domestic violence, what does the thesaurus tell me is the best word or phrase to use in my search?

2) I'm searching Sociofile for citations to articles on the socialization problems facing children born with Downs Syndrome. I've looked in the thesaurus and found that the phrase Downs Syndrome is a good search phrase to use, but my search results aren't giving me enough information. According to the thesaurus, what are the related terms I should search with?

3) In Sociofile, if I'm searching for citations to articles about physical abuse between husbands and wives, what one thesaurus word or phrase focuses most specifically to my topic?

Figure 11 Guide to the Literature Assignment

Final Project: Guide to the Literature

Your assignment is to compile a descriptive and evaluative guide to the **basic information sources** for a major subject area in the academic discipline of your choice. This guide, or pathfinder, should be an organized listing and description of a variety of English language sources of information on your selected topic. It should be designed to help another individual determine which basic sources are best to consult in the early stages of research. The guide is *not* meant to be an exhaustive bibliography on your subject; rather, the sources included in the guide should assist a researcher in developing his or her own comprehensive list of sources.

Choose to work within whatever academic discipline you prefer, i.e., literature, political science, sociology, Asian studies, zoology, accounting, etc. Depending on the discipline you choose, you might need to broaden or narrow your topic. For example, if you choose sociology as your discipline, you should probably concentrate on a specialty within that discipline, such as criminology. The academic discipline should *be neither too broad nor too narrow*. It is recommended that your choice have a substantial body of readily accessible literature. Please consult with me in advance if you have any questions about topic selection.

Statement of Scope
At the beginning of your pathfinder, you should write a brief statement of scope. This should be one or two paragraphs that clearly define your topic and present other introductory or preliminary information. Assume that the audience for your guide to the literature are freshman or sophomore majors in the given field.

Organization
If the guide is not organized effectively, it will not be of much assistance to the user. While there is no one best way to organize information for all subjects, each of the following types of sources are likely to be included in a complete guide:
- Guides/Handbooks
- Bibliographies
- Biographical Dictionaries
- Subject-Specific Encyclopedias and Dictionaries
- Major Periodicals in the Field
- Major Periodical Indexes and Abstracts (both print and electronic)
- Statistical Sources (both print and electronic)
- Internet Sources
- Scholarly/Professional Association or Organizations
- Other Relevant Sources

Evaluative Annotations
Besides citing the important works, you are expected to write a brief evaluative annotation. This is an essential component of the guide, because these annotations will assist the audience in evaluating the usefulness of the work. Your recommendations are fine but you may also support them with expert opinion, i.e., reviews, other guides, etc. Obviously, in order to evaluate these sources, you will need to look at them. It is important, therefore, that the University libraries own this information. The following are suggested areas of commentary:
- Explain the main purpose of the work.
- Briefly describe the contents.
- Indicate the possible audience for the work.

Figure 11 Continued

- Comment on special features.
- Comment on strengths, weaknesses, or biases.

Format
The length of the guide will depend on the subject you select as well as the length of your annotations. **Four pages, typed, is a reasonable minimum and eight pages maximum.** Please cite the source you used to locate each work listed in your guide. Footnotes or endnotes should conform to the Turabian style manual.

Deadline
All guides are due by **NOON, Tuesday, December 6. Late guides will not be accepted.** The guide counts as 1/3 of your grade for the course and must be submitted to receive a passing grade in the class.

REFERENCES

1. Wilson, Lizabeth A. "Changing Users: Bibliographic Instruction for Whom?" In *The Evolving Educational Mission of the Library,* edited by Betsy Baker and Mary Ellen Litzinger, 20–53. Chicago: Association of College and Research Libraries, 1992.
2. Wittkopf, Barbara. "A Look at the State of BI Credit Courses in ARL-Member Libraries." *Research Strategies* 9 (Fall 1991): 162–163.
3. Hensley, Randall. "Teaching Methods." In *Sourcebook for Bibliographic Instruction,* 29–44. Chicago: Association of College and Research Libraries, 1993.
4. Roberts, Anne. F., and Susan G. Blandy. *Library Instruction for Librarians,* 2nd revised ed. Englewood, CO: Libraries Unlimited, 1989.
5. Grassian, Esther. "Setting Up and Managing a BI Program." In *Sourcebook for Bibliographic Instruction, 59–75.* Chicago: Association of College and Research Libraries, 1993.
6. Adams, Mignon S., and Jacquelyn M. Morris. *Teaching Library Skills for Academic Credit.* Phoenix: Oryx Press, 1985. Although in need of updating, this source provides a comprehensive look at the process of creating a credit course and offers numerous descriptions of credit courses offered by academic libraries across the country.
7. Wittkopf, 1991.
8. See Constance A. Mellon's "Process Not Product in Course-Integrated Instruction: A Generic Model of Library Research," *College and Research Libraries* 45 (November 1984): 471–478; David Kohn and Lizabeth A. Wilson's "Effectiveness of Course-Integrated Bibliographic Instruction in Improving Coursework," *RQ* 26 (Winter 1986): 206–211; and Lori Arp and Lizabeth A. Wilson's "Structures of Bibliographic Instruction Programs: A Continuum for Planning," *Reference Librarian* 24 (1989): 25–34.
9. Lippincott, Joan K. "End-User Instruction: Emphasis on Concepts." In *Conceptual Frameworks for Bibliographic Education: Theory into Practice,* edited by Mary Reichel and Mary Ann Ramey, 183–191. Littleton, CO: Libraries Unlimited, 1987.
10. Oberman, Cerise. "Avoiding the Cereal Syndrome, or Critical Thinking in the Electronic Environment." *Library Trends* 39 (Winter 1991): 189–202.

11. Arp, Lori. "An Introduction to Learning Theory." In *Sourcebook for Bibliographic Instruction,* 5–15. Chicago: Association of College and Research Libraries, 1993.

12. Grunland, Norman E. *How to Write and Use Instructional Objectives,* 4th ed. New York: Macmillan, 1991.

13. ACRL/BIS Task Force on Model Statement of Objectives. "Model Statement of Objectives for Academic Bibliographic Instruction." *College and Research Libraries News* 48 (May 1987): 256–261. Examples of how academic libraries have adapted the Model Statement to create course objectives are available in the 1991 ACRL publication, *Read This First: An Owner's Guide to the New Model Statement of Objectives for Academic Bibliographic Instruction,* edited by Carolyn Dusenbury et al.

14. Kobelski, Pamela, and Mary Reichel. "Conceptual Frameworks for Bibliographic Instruction." In *Conceptual Frameworks for Bibliographic Education: Theory into Practice,* edited by Mary Reichel and Mary Ann Ramey, 3–12. Littleton, CO: Libraries Unlimited, 1987. Other frameworks suitable for an electronic information literacy course are described in Ilene F. Rockman's "Teaching About the Internet: The Formal Course Option," *Reference Librarian* 39 (1993): 65–75; and Mary H. Huston and Cerise Oberman's "Making Communication: A Theoretical Framework for Educating End-Users of Online Bibliographic Information Retrieval Systems," *Reference Librarian* 24 (1989): 199–211.

15. Adams, Mignon S. "Evaluation." In *Sourcebook for Bibliographic Instruction,* 45–57. Chicago: Association of College and Research Libraries, 1993.

9 DESIGNING THE ELECTRONIC CLASSROOM

Laurel Adams
New Mexico State University Library

WHY ELECTRONIC CLASSROOMS?

Teaching patrons one-on-one, at the reference desk, to use electronic resources places a heavy demand on personnel. Librarians have learned to cope with the demand by providing group instruction. However, simply demonstrating software to a group of patrons is no longer sufficient for teaching information-seeking skills in an increasingly technological environment. In fact, it has been compared to asking computer science instructors to teach classes without computers.[1] Providing students with hands-on experience during instruction is essential if they are to transform class content into mastery.

Teaching methods in academic classrooms are changing. There is an emerging focus on the student-teacher relationship and the role of collaboration. Technology is being used to foster collaboration and, at least in the classroom, has not dehumanized the process of relating.[2] Libraries need to keep pace with these changing educational methods if they want to develop or maintain an influential role in the learning process. One pitfall, however, is the tendency to implement technology for its own sake. Electronic classrooms should be designed for effective teaching, not for applying new technologies or imparting new "computer skills." According to W. Gilbert,[3] instructors ought to ask, "[can] my goals for this class be better accomplished using collaborative techniques and improved communication between the students, myself, and their classmates?"

When administrators decide to add an electronic classroom to their facilities, they must plan carefully for the many facets of classroom design. The following chapter lays out questions and issues that planners will want to consider.

NEW FACILITIES OR RENOVATIONS

It is important to begin lab design by assessing specific intended uses since different applications warrant specific considerations regarding furniture, hardware, and equipment. For instance, planners need to know if the lab will be used for short bibliographic instruction sessions, technology/literacy courses for credit, or computer resources for students. Because there are so many specialized areas of facility planning, it is wise to hire a consultant or involve others with expertise in fields such as heating, ventilation, air condition (HVAC), computer systems, and electrical systems. Also, a committee comprised of representatives of interested groups, such as the computer center, physical plant, facilities coordinators, and teaching faculty, can serve as advocates for developing and improving classrooms and can assist in the planning stages.

Electronic classrooms require 700–1,200 square feet for 20–30 computer stations. Bibliographic instruction classrooms in older buildings are often renovations of small corners of libraries. They were not designed with technology in mind. Consequently, libraries renovating these facilities into electronic classrooms will be limited by their own circumstances as well as the financial resources designated for the project.

The location of the lab should be chosen with regard to traffic flow and arranged with the door at the rear of the room. If possible, place it close to the entrance of the building so that classes moving to and from the lab do not disrupt other library activities.

BUILDING CODES AND STANDARDS

Clabaugh, *et al.*[4] provides a bibliography of codes and standards guides and a list of relevant regulation and code agencies. Of great concern is the interpretation of and conformance to the Americans with Disabilities Act (ADA) standards. "Accessible and reasonable accommodation is mandated in new construction and facility renovation unless the cost of the addition or renovation becomes an undue hardship."[5] *Undue hardship* is difficult to define but may be understood as constituting a portion of the budget so significant that completing the project with the remaining resources is impossible. Also, B. Duggan states that if the resources to be housed in the lab are accessible elsewhere in the facility to people with disabilities, accommodating it to ADA specifications may not be required. Institutions should consult either the UFSAS (Uniform Federal Accessibility Standards) or the ADAAG (Americans with Disabilities Act Accessibility Guidelines). In addition, check for State mandated standards to which facility planners must adhere.

There are certain basic features which will facilitate access by persons with disabilities. Doorways should be at least 36" wide. There should be space, five feet in diameter, inside the lab so that wheel chairs can be turned around. For specific types of disabilities, labs may include Braille signs, optical character recognition apparatus, over-sized keyboards, or joysticks. For the hearing impaired, units may be equipped with *assisted listening devices,* whereby audio from the sound system is transmitted electronically to transducers located at select computer stations. For the vision impaired, it is recommended that high-contrast colors be chosen for decor and, to avoid glare, that moderate lighting levels be maintained.

Some general room standards may be helpful to designers in the early stages. For rooms with a capacity of 50 occupants or fewer, one door is sufficient. It should have a shatter resistant, tinted glass panel so that no one is injured if it swings unexpectedly. It should be placed, recessed into the room if possible, so that it does not open into either a hallway or a primary flow of traffic. Doors with levers as handles are easier for disabled people to open than ones with knobs.

Ceiling heights influence air flow and air-conditioning requirements. For a room designed to hold up to 20 students, an eight-foot ceiling is adequate. For rooms with a 20–50 person capacity, plan for a ten-foot ceiling. Larger rooms may require a distance of twelve feet from the ceiling to the floor.[4]

Windows should be at the sides of the room, not the rear or front. Window treatments should block out light. Possible types include venetian blinds, roller blinds, or drapes. If the room does not have windows, give careful attention to interior finishes and decor so that it will be visually appealing and conducive to learning.

OUTFITTING THE LAB

FURNITURE

Desks: Labs are generally designed to hold 25–50 people with one or two students to a computer station. When planning for two people per station, be sure two chairs can fit easily under desks. While some recommend the standard height of 29"–30" for desks, others assert that the optimum height for manipulating the keyboard and mouse is 24"–26".[5] There should be at least 24" of leg room beneath the desk and 22"–30" on the surface for elbow room, manuals, and note-taking. Desks should have sides that extend to the floor and have provisions for covering wiring. "[Desks] need to protect sensitive equipment, provide platforms on which the equipment will operate, house electrical boxes and on/off switches, house a circuit breaker, and hide as much wiring as possible."[6]

Cases for disk drives must be ventilated, have holes for power cords and cables, and have space for keyboards and monitors. Some monitor platforms are adjustable, enabling the viewer to tip the monitor to an appropriate angle. "The ideal position for computer use places the nose level with the computer screen, feet firmly on the ground, and elbows at 90%".[5] Some desks house the monitors within their tabletops so that students look down into them. This provides more space for note-taking and, when desks have been arranged in forward-facing rows, an unobstructed line of sight to the teacher's station at the front of the room. Others contest these inset monitors as prone to glare and difficult to read.

As for the instructor's station, a well-equipped post includes a desk, computer stand, monitor stand, shelves for software and other materials, a closet nearby for miscellaneous supplies, and, possibly, a podium.

Arranging Desks: Different room arrangements afford unique advantages and disadvantages and are a matter of preference and teaching style. If desks are situated in certain angles near windows, daylight can wash out monitor images. Other arrays, window treatments, or glare screens can rectify the problem. A popular configuration is to line the desks along the perimeter. This allows for greater traffic flow through the center of the room and away from wires, cables, and hardware. Also, instructors can walk freely between stations to view work on monitors over students' shoulders. Long tables placed in the center of the room can serve as areas for students to finish up work or wait for stations to be vacated. The disadvantage of this arrangement, however, is that students must turn away from their monitors in order to see the instructor. This makes taking notes difficult since the writing surface is at their backs.

Traditional forward-facing rows let students look past their monitors to the instructor and back again with relative ease. They can take notes and compare their work with other students or with examples projected at the front of the room. This configuration can, however, inhibit traffic flow as students move in and out of their computers. Wires are also more likely to be tripped over or inadvertently dislodged if not carefully hidden and protected. Lastly, it is more difficult to track student work when monitors face away from the instructor.

Variations on these layouts can allow designers to utilize limited spaces and still create effective teaching environments. Horseshoe or U-shaped seating schemes, double oval schemes, desk cluster schemes, and V-shaped cluster schemes are also options. Others design labs with standard rows of desks at the center and computers at the periphery so that lecture and instruction take place prior to student practice. S. Manual and J.D. Quest[7] include seating diagrams, total area required for each design, area per station required, travel distance within the lab, and performance ratings of lab designs.

Planners should visit labs with various arrangements, preferably during instruction sessions. This will help them to weigh the pros and cons of each and select one that will complement the teaching styles of the instructors in their own libraries.

Chairs: Rooms with a capacity under 50 should have movable seating; ten percent of the stations should be offset to the left for left-handed people; and four percent of the stations should be wheelchair accessible.[4] Armless swivel chairs, adjustable for height and back support, ought to have casters appropriate for the surface, either tile or carpet, so that the chairs can roll. Chairs that swivel allow students to face the teacher who may be checking work on computer screens at student stations or instructing from any of several points in the lab. The 0-1-2-3 guide to selecting chairs maintains that when considering padding, none is necessary for short durations of sitting, 1" is required for 30–60 minutes, 2" provides adequate comfort for periods of one to two hours, and anything longer warrants 3" of padding.[5]

WHITE BOARDS AND SCREENS

Although some people experience a chemical sensitivity to the markers used on *white boards,* they are preferable to chalk boards which generate high levels of dust that damage hard drives and other computer equipment. Select a board with a flat matte finish as this minimizes glare. As projection surfaces, these yield good picture quality and offer the widest viewing angle (45 percent) on each side of the center viewing line. The trade-offs for the brighter images produced on *beaded, gain,* and *lenticular* projection screens are the narrower viewing angles and potential for *hot spots* (bright spots) in the image. These screens may be preferable to white boards, however, when ambient light is difficult to eliminate.

Keystoning, or the trapezoidal appearance of images on screen, can be remedied in some projectors by adjusting their bases, or, if this is not a feature of the unit, by pulling the bottom of the screen outward from the wall. Tilting the screen is adequate for computer generated images but it will distort video images. Purchasing an adjustable projector is preferable.

LIGHTING

In order to produce images with the best clarity possible, lighting must be adjustable enough to allow areas around screens to be darkened considerably. Some projectors require a completely darkened room for satisfactory image quality. However, students then have difficulty taking notes. Zoned dimmers are the best solution but also the most expensive. An alternative is to place a number of incandescent lights among the florescent ones so that, when the latter are off, there is still adequate light for note-taking. Lighting should generally fall between 50–60 foot-candles and should be reducible to 5–10 foot-candles over seating areas.[4] Teachers will be able to refer to notes and outlines if a concentrated light source shines on a small area of the instructor's station. In labs designed for more than 50 students, white boards illuminated at 75 foot-candles will facilitate viewing from the rear of the room.

WALLS

When choosing finishes, consider their *reflectance values.* Paints, vinyl coverings, and laminates can diminish or enhance ambient light as needed. Clabaugh[4] suggests acceptable ranges for these values and notes that they can be found in charts and on product samples. Durability is another quality to consider when choosing finishes as it is likely that items such as book and computer carts will be brought in and out of the lab and may bump and damage some surfaces. Chair rails in rooms with movable seating and base guards along the walls also assist in preserving the appearance of the lab.

ACOUSTICS

The STC (Sound Transmission Coefficient) for the lab should be no less than 50. This will allow students to hear over the hum of computer equipment, HVAC systems, or other noises in the library. Carpet will improve the acoustical quality of the room, but static electricity, a phenomena most prevalent in dryer climates, can cause equipment to short. Some cope with this problem by spraying the carpet with carpet guard or a fabric softener and water mixture two or three times a week.[6] Others purchase static-free tile or linoleum and accommodate for noise by inserting acoustical tiles in ceilings. Tiles are plaster board or gypsum and are arranged in a U-shape to optimize sound absorption. The number of tiles required to reduce noise to an acceptable level will depend on the height of the room.

Noise levels can also be controlled by locating the lab away from elevators or other machinery and by the careful selection and placement of lab equipment. For instance, noise covers are available for dot-matrix printers. Printers of any type may be positioned at the rear of the lab or in recessed areas designated for them so that associated noises and activities are isolated.

Sound systems may be in order for larger rooms. These typically include speakers, a microphone, an amplifier, and an equalizer. Rooms can be equipped with high-quality radio microphones that tend to deflect background noises such as projector fans or software-generated computer sounds. Some teachers prefer these systems as they allow them to move freely about while still amplifying their voices. The cardioid microphone, suspended from a boom over the instructor's station, is an alternative that registers both computer and voice.

ENVIRONMENTAL CONTROLS

Air circulation rates, temperature, and humidity need to be considered when designing the classroom. An American Society of Heating, Refrigeration, and Airconditioning Engineers' standard determines the adequate number of air changes per hour within a room. Many recommend installing ceiling fans in addition to HVAC systems to keep air moving, especially in smaller classrooms. The temperature should be between 50–90°F, with optimum hardware efficiency occurring at 65–75°F. Relative humidity levels can range from 20–80 percent and will be optimum at 30–50 percent.[6]

ACCESSORIES

Other items may be purchased for the lab if warranted by the type of instruction intended. For instance, if the lab is to be used for extended classes, foot-rests, copy holders, or task lighting may be useful. Racks for promotional and informational materials should be included. A phone in the lab is helpful in ensuring the problems with the facility or equipment will be reported quickly. Basic items, such as trash containers and exit signs, should not be overlooked.

ELECTRONIC EQUIPMENT

PROJECTION EQUIPMENT

LCD vs. CRT Projection Equipment: The quality of a projected image can ultimately enhance or diminish the effectiveness of the electronic classroom as a learning environment and the projection equipment may be the single most expensive component in designing an electronic classroom. What follows are issues to be considered with care when deciding between cathode ray tube (CRT) and liquid crystal display (LCD) technology.

Motion Video: Motion video projected through a CRT tends to be more uniform and have higher resolution than motion video through some LCD units. Ensure that the unit's pixel response time is less than 50 milliseconds for both motion video and computer animation applications. At response times greater than 75 milliseconds, mouse pointers will fade from the screen. Some LCD panels can have rapid pixel response times and display computer animation well, but may not support the National Television Standard Code for video images.

Portability: LCD panels are simpler to set up and more easily transported compared to bulkier CRT projectors which require *convergence adjustments* when they are moved or fall out of alignment. For ceiling-mounted CRT projectors, a ladder is needed to make modifications.

Image Quality: CRTs generally produce brighter images and are more effective in larger rooms or in rooms that cannot be fully darkened than LCDs which rely on overhead projectors for light sources. The unit of measure for the brightness of video projection systems is in *lumens* but can be assessed in different ways. The resulting values cannot always be compared. Unless the rating method is listed as American National Standard Institute, it is best to test equipment to compare actual brightness. Overhead projectors chosen for use with LCDs should cast between 2,700 and 3,000 lumens.[8]

Active matrix is a newer technology used in CRTs for more rapid response and higher contrast in color displays. Additionally, CRTs can have either *fixed* or *variable convergence lengths*. The former indicates that the image always appears at a fixed distance from the projector. Consequently, the screen must always be positioned at the same distance from the projector and the image size cannot be varied. In CRTs with variable convergence lengths, moving the projector forward and backward reduces and enlarges the image on the screen.

Another important consideration for CRT units is the range of *scanning frequencies* the projector can accept from the computer. Different computers and video equipment have different scanning rates. One convenient alternative is a multi-scan video projector that automatically adjusts to the correct frequency from the computer. Projectors with lower frequencies can be adapted for use with higher frequency computers by attaching a converter that lowers the signal to the projector's range, but the image quality and resolution capacities of the computer will be diminished in the display.

Cost: LCD panel and overhead projector are generally priced between five and seven thousand dollars while low-end CRT projectors start at nine thousand, not including the cost of installation. The choice between LCD and CRT technology should not be made simply on the basis of cost, but with regard for how and where it will be used.

REAR OR FRONT PROJECTION

Rear projection allows the positioning of a teacher in front of the screen without blocking the image projection and is effective in rooms where ambient light can hamper image clarity. However, the appropriate distance of the projector to the screen must be allotted or mirrors and lenses must be carefully utilized to duplicate the distance. Rear projection systems can be purchased as single units to avoid using extra space or mirrors, but they tend to be bulky and do not enhance the 50 percent viewing angle generally afforded by this type of projection system

Front projection tends to offer a wider viewing angle if appropriate screens are used; computer-generated text will be brighter and have greater resolution. Some front projection systems can be mounted from the ceiling to maintain an open path from the projector to the screen. It will not be necessary to climb a ladder for making adjustments if a unit with a remote control is purchased.

Regardless of the direction of projection, the distance between the farthest viewer and the screen should be no greater than six times the screen width. Some recommend reducing the distance to no more than four times the screen width; they anticipate that improvements in projection technology will lead to more sophisticated applications of electronic projection[4] and, presumably, produce images with levels of detail that can be appreciated only at closer distances.

INTEGRATED CONTROL SYSTEMS

Integrated control systems can facilitate the use of various projectors, videocassette players, computers, and lights from the instructor's station. These can be either configurable software, such as AMX, Video Director, or Creston control systems, or can be programmed microcomputers that display a series of menu choices when the instructor begins. Much of the software allows instructors to set up individual profiles that can be reused later. A system now being marketed by Extron has been designed to "control all room technology functions and to provide a Knowledge-Based Help System that automatically pages a technician when help is required."[8]

MONITORS

Studies on emission rates from video display terminals have not confirmed health risks, but some researchers have suggested that exposure to extremely low frequency (ELF) and very low frequency radiation may cause diseases such as leukemia and brain tumors. Monitors should emit no more than 2.5 milligauss (measured by a gaussmeter) at a distance of 20 centimeters. Since no official standard exists at this time, many computer manufacturers conform to this guideline, established by the Swedish National Board for Measurement, known as MPRII.[9] "[Emissions] are especially significant in laboratories where 20–30 machines are in use at one time. Wise administrators will investigate available research and standards concerning these waves and work to mitigate their effect."[10]

WIRING

Two types of wiring will be necessary for the lab: network cable and 110-volt alternating current wire. Lay network cable so that rooms need as few feet as possible since increased distances between computers and servers slow data transmission and often necessitate additional equipment to enhance efficiency. Networks should not be located in high-voltage areas. Sensitive ethernet cables will be best protected beneath the floors, but sub-floor utilities are costly and difficult to access for maintenance. Raceways, conduits, and boxes fastened to the floor create uneven surfaces and make moving equipment troublesome. Locating wiring within the walls is most preferable.

An adequate number of outlets, mounted 18"–24" inches from the floor, should be available in the lab. It has been suggested that an addition 20–40 percent be added to accommodate future needs.[4] The lab should withstand the simultaneous start-up of all machines. Dedicated lines are essential for servers and other heavy equipment, but are not required for each computer.[10] Include several circuits, one for the instructor's station, one for each group of ten computers, one for overhead lights, one to turn all student monitors on or off at once from the instructor's station, and extras for expanding as needed.

Provisions must be made for power spikes, brown-outs, and blackouts. It is not enough simply to equip each circuit with a breaker since cutting the power instantly can cause information loss or disk damage. *Surge protectors* can diminish risk but most systems designers advocate using an Uninterruptible Power Supply (UPS) despite higher costs that range between $300 and $2,000. One UPS will serve up to ten computers and will direct power to them during a brown-out. In the event of a blackout, it can keep computers running up to 30 minutes, furnishing time to save work-in-progress and shut down the system.[11]

SOFTWARE

"Lectureware" is making teaching with technology increasingly sophisticated. Integrated control systems ideally allow "bidirectional communications"[3] between and among teachers and students. For example, "[s]oftware is available which permits an instructor to quickly assess the level or preparedness of the class by asking a question and receiving anonymous responses from all students, not just the traditional hand-raisers."[3] Images on the students' or instructor's screen should be projectable to either the instructor's monitor, the white board, or to any or all other student monitors. Software, such as LANSchool, provides these features and is a better alternative than using circuits to turn off student monitors. Also within the teacher's control is the ability to switch from the computer monitor to the overhead projector, VCR, or perhaps a live video camera focused on print resources or specimens.

In order to learn the various facts of database searching, students should all be able to work in the same database simultaneously. Therefore, it is important that networked resources, such as the Internet, public access catalogs, or electronic indexes, be accessed from all stations at once in the classroom. This also allows the instructor to work through specific examples and keep all class members paced with one another. However, license requirements on electronic resources must be observed. Lab designers are encouraged to investigate educational discounts and training clauses when using restricted resources. If users access databases via a modem, the lab will need to be outfitted with telephone connections. If the network goes down, all networked resources become inaccessible. Consequently, it is advisable to have a CD-ROM drive and extra disks at the instructor's station so that a scheduled class can minimally see these resources demonstrated on the projection system.

Many electronic indexes and other applications now run in both DOS and Windows environments. Depending on current or anticipated applications, planners may want to include Windows.

SECURITY

Security risks fall within six general areas: fire, disaster, theft, vandalism, copyright, and virus For fire protection, supply labs with appropriate extinguishers, not water or powder-based since these cause extensive damage to expensive equipment. Consider smoke alarms that register levels of humidity or temperature falling outside acceptable ranges so that conditions that can damage costly equipment are discovered as soon as possible. A fire door designed to last for two hours is also recommended. Strategies for disaster prevention will entail adding extra precautions, such as measures against floods or earthquakes, and will differ according to the risk associated with the region.

Several precautions against theft are available. Steel cables can secure individual components to desks and floors. Electronic cables and alarmed power strips are designed to activate if lines are cut or plugs are disconnected. Simple dissuasions include engraving or stenciling hardware with identification numbers. A newer and more difficult form of theft to thwart is the cracking of hard drives and removal of expansion boards, video cards, and other components. For protection against vandalism, designers may decide to include other security measures, such as alarmed doors and windows, motion detectors, card-key systems, or surveillance cameras. Choose the security system carefully if the lab has a false ceiling, since these ceilings have reportedly been access points for thieves at some institutions.

Generally, copyright restrictions are difficult, if not impossible, to enforce, but it is important to show a good faith effort towards restricting improper use of copyrighted resources. Signs should be posted within the lab explaining that users are responsible for knowing and complying with copyright restrictions. "The library's role as a computer resource center carries with it the responsibility to model ethical computer behavior. This includes, at least, the establishment and enforcement of policies regarding software use and copying."[12] Viruses also pose a security risk. Each CPU should have virus-checking software that users cannot bypass when booting the system.

ESTIMATING COSTS

Costs will differ greatly but should account for system support and training. Designers may choose to hire a single contractor for the job or hire contractors with expertise in specialized areas. Some important factors that will influence the installation cost are the types of ceilings, location of cable, and the ease of hooking up components. Take advantage of contractors that provide free site surveys when estimating costs and ask about educational discounts and warranties. Warranties may or may not include parts and labor or temporary replacements for broken equipment.

Establish a plan to cover maintenance and replacement costs. Life-cycle funding, a concept used widely with interior furnishings, is now being applied to equipment. Creating a schedule to resell equipment around the three to five year mark can help administrators "realize the maximum benefit from their initial investment."[4]

MANAGING THE CLASSROOM

The development of a policies and procedures statement will simplify electronic classroom management for administrators. This document should include methods for scheduling the classroom, priorities for groups and uses, lists of people who will have access to the room, and standards for software and hardware support.[13] Campus-wide groups may be organized to examine these issues, as well as resource distribution and use patterns, as they relate to the rest of the university. It is also important to plan training strategies to assist faculty in making the most of the room's capabilities. This should start with an orientation to the basics, such as how to boot the system, use the lab according to policy, handle problems with the facility or equipment, find miscellaneous supplies, and use the integrated control systems and application software. Trainers should also be taught successful teaching strategies for electronic environments so they may integrate the technology into their teaching methods.

Administrators should devise a maintenance plan and systems technicians should create a troubleshooting guide. Someone must be designated to maintain a detailed inventory list and be responsible for the security of the lab. Signs should be posted inside and out indicating who should be notified when problems arise. Downtime for broken components can be minimized by keeping a small stock of replacement equipment, such as keyboards and monitors, that can be quickly and easily changed.

Promotional campaigns can announce the opening dates of the new labs and the services they offer. Publishing a regular newsletter for the lab with upcoming classes, new resources, and helpful hints can be an effective way to enhance the library's visibility in the institution.[12]

New computer classrooms reportedly tend to be filled 70–90 percent of the schedulable time with seating capacity at 65–75 percent. The impact of an electronic classroom can be overwhelming, if unanticipated. Usually, instructional programs will become stronger and more popular. Increased demand for instruction will increase the resources required to sustain programs and facilities. Planners may find electronic classrooms are so well received that their expertise will be called upon to design others.

REFERENCES

1. Wiggins, M. E. and D. H. Howard. (1993, July). "Developing Support Facilities for BYU's Bibliographic Instruction Program." *The Journal of Academic Librarianship,* 19(3): 144–148.
2. Wilson, D. L. (1993, March 17). "Universities Wrestle with the Design of Tomorrow's High-Tech Classroom."*The Chronicle of Higher Education*: A19–A20.
3. Gilbert, W. (1991, Fall). "The AT&T Teaching Theater at

the University of Maryland at College Park." *SIGUCCS Newsletter, 21*(3): 17–19.

4. Clabaugh, S. (Ed.), R. L. Allen, D. K. Ault, J. T. Bowen, B. B. DeWitt, J. Francis, J. P. Kerstetter, and R. T. Sodergren. (1993). *Design of General Purpose Classrooms, Lecture Halls, and Seminar Rooms* (2nd ed.), College Park, MD: Educational Technology Center, University of Maryland.

5. Duggan, B. (1994, September). "A Measures Approach to Microcomputer Lab Design." *Tech Trends, 39*(4): 24–28.

6. Moran, T. (1987, March). "The Ideal Computer Lab from Floor to Ceiling." *Tech Trends 32*(2): 18–20.

7. Manuel, S. and J. D. Quest. (1988, July). "Curriculum and Environment Interact." *AS&U Facility Planning Guide, 60*(11): 22–23.

8. Conway, K. (1994). "Master Classrooms: Classroom Design with Technology in Mind. In Institute for Academic Technology," *Classroom Design with Technology in Mind Videorecording* [Supplementary Reading Booklet] (pp. 1–15). Durham, NC: Author.

9. McKimmie, T. and J. Smith. (1994, September). "The ELF in Your Library." *Computers in Libraries, 14*(2): 16–20.

10. Ross, T. W. (1992, September). "A Principle's Guide to ILS Facilities Installation." *Educational Technology, 32*(9): 33–35.

11. Landt, C. (1994, June 16). Surge Protectors [E-mail to Laural Adams], [Online]. Available E-mail: LADAMS@lib.nmsu.edu

12. Bunson, S. (1988, August). "Design of an IMC Micro Center." *Educational Technology, 28*(8): 29–32.

13. Barker, B. O. and B. R. Harris. (1993). "Establishing and Using an Electronic Classroom: The Western Illinois University Experience." (ERIC Document Reproduction Service No. ED 360 958).

ADDITIONAL READING

Blackett, A. and B. Stanfield. (1994, Spring). A Planner's Guide to Tomorrow's Classrooms. *Planning for Higher Education, 22*: 25–31.

Duesterhoeft, D. (1993, Fall). The Electronic Classroom [Discussion]. Bibliographic Instruction Discussion List [Online]. Available E-mail: BI-L@BINGVMB.cc.binghamton.edu

Janicke, L. (1994). Designing an Electronic Library Classroom:

An Annotated Bibliography, [Online]. Available http://www.ed.uiuc.edu/EdPsy-387Lisa-Janicke/Abstracts.html

Knirk, F. G. (1987). Instructional Facilities for the Information Age. (ERIC Document Reproduction Service No. ED 296 734)

Noe, M. A. (1983, May). Planning a Microcomputer Lab. *School Business Affairs, 49*(5): 56, 70.

Seilheimer, S. D. (n.d.) A Methodical Approach to the Creation, Operation, and Enhancement of a General-Use Microcomputer Laboratory. *Educational Technology, 28*(5): 11–16.

Vasi, J. and C. La Guardia. (1992, March). Setting Up CD-ROM Work Areas. Part 1: Ergonomic Considerations, User Furniture, Location. *CD-ROM Professional, 5*(2): 44–46.

10 MANAGING ELECTRONIC INFORMATION LITERACY EDUCATION

Charles T. Townley
New Mexico State University Library
and
R. David Myers
New Mexico State University Library

INTRODUCTION

Librarians have an extraordinary opportunity to contribute to the information literacy of American college graduates. For more than a century, academic librarians have worked to supply printed information needed for teaching and learning. As a result, librarians have a clear understanding of scholarly information and know how to evaluate it. As information providers, they are respected throughout the academy. In recent years, librarians have begun to play a more dynamic role by regularly helping faculty improve the development of student information skills through their course work, often providing instruction to assure basic skills and developing expert skills in specific disciplines.

For librarians to succeed as teachers of information literacy, library administrations will need to play an active role in modifying professional roles. Administrators will have to create an environment where librarians can address scholarly information in all formats so that the whole information spectrum is presented, especially electronic information,[1] and librarians will have to work to expand their direct role in teaching information literacy. While both of these changes are evolutionary, together they constitute a new paradigm for libraries and higher education.[2]

This process of change is already well under way. Several professional organizations have taken steps to facilitate the change. The American Library Association (ALA) has adopted guidelines that suggest librarians and their libraries undertake information literacy programs. The Coalition of Networked Information,[3] a cooperative of the Association of Research Libraries, CAUSE, and EDUCOM, is working to assure the emergence of high-quality information literacy programs (FNCNI Goals). This chapter contributes to a growing literature by exploring practical applications and outcomes for teaching electronic information literacy.

The purpose of this chapter is to suggest the means of managing education for electronic information literacy from an administrative perspective with a particular eye toward desired outcomes. Topics to be covered include leadership, planning and marketing, staffing, budgeting, and evaluating. Examples are provided throughout to suggest areas of opportunity and successful application. Please note that the example for this section will be the ALA Guidelines on Information Literacy.

ALA Policy 52.6—Instruction in the use of libraries

In order to assist individuals in the independent information retrieval process basic to daily living in a democratic society, the American Library Association encourages all libraries to include instruction in the use of libraries as one of the primary goals of service. Libraries of all types share the responsibility to educate users in successful information location, beginning with their childhood years and continuing the education process throughout their years of professional and personal growth.

LEADERSHIP

For the library's role in advancing electronic information literacy to succeed, it must enjoy strong support and commitment from library administration. Support must then be developed among the university faculty, students, and academic administration. Library administrators must help develop a core group of librarians to undertake electronic information literacy as one of their primary responsibilities. Administrators must assume the leadership role by assessing academic needs, creating a plan that addresses those needs, and sharing that plan among library personnel, faculty, students, and academic administrators.

The first step in developing any plan is to assess interest in and motivation to achieve electronic information literacy. Studying the institutional mission and goals, accreditation requirements, and general education requirements reveals underlying needs for information literacy education. These statements often provide strong endorsement for the concepts of academic outcomes and life-long learning. Careful study of them will suggest strategies for involving electronic information literacy.

It is also useful to begin soliciting support from academic administrators and university faculty. Without active support for information literacy on the part of academic administrators, the struggle for a viable program (especially in terms of financial support) will be difficult. Early and active participation by all faculty will help assure curricular approval. It will also provide a powerful support group when the academic administration is approached for institutional and financial support.

Simultaneously, library administrators should make an assessment of student information skills, use, and satisfaction as part of a needs assessment. At New Mexico State University (NMSU), for example, it is known that less than half of entering freshmen can correctly describe how to identify and borrow a book from the University library. Less than 40 percent have enough computer experience to use an electronic database and less than 30 percent are able to describe how to identify and copy a periodical article. These figures demonstrate a clear need for improving electronic information literacy.

Similarly, user behavior and satisfaction describe areas of instructional need. When asked what information resources were used on their last paper or project, NMSU students suggest that printed material is their primary source. They also indicate that other information resources, such as personal datafiles and online information, are increasingly used. These information sources supplement each other and are perceived to be complementary. Satisfaction, on the other hand, appears to decline as unskilled people increase their efforts to acquire information. At NMSU, users often report finding less than 30 percent of what they want despite the fact that the library owns 70 percent of materials cited in faculty publications. Repeated failure at the terminal and at the shelf caused by lack of information search skills generates this dissatisfaction.

In addition to quantitative assessments of need, careful attention must also be paid to qualitative assessment. It is often available in the form of comments from librarians, advisory groups, faculty, and students. Qualitative information provides the detail needed to design a strong vision for electronic information literacy. Beginners may want to learn only how to access electronic information resources through a common interface. Commuters may want to learn dial-in techniques. Faculty and graduate students may need to master the key information elements in the esoteric databases of their discipline. All users may desire to seek assistance when it is needed in a new area of interest.[4]

The final part of the needs assessment is developing an awareness of the strengths and weaknesses of available technologies and other environmental factors. Does, for example, the institution have or intend to install a comprehensive telecommunications network? What technologies will be supported on this network? Is support provided for non-traditional instructional technologies? Is the overall financial forecast good, fair, or poor? Is distance education or some other technology-intensive program being started? In other words, what are the resources of the institution that affect the ability to master information literacy.

With a needs assessment completed, administrators need to define a plan for teaching electronic information literacy at their institution. The plan should address educational needs, institutional support, and outcomes. It should reflect the interests and concerns of librarians and it should be succinct. The plan for electronic information literacy should be a key part of general strategic planning for the library. It should be understandable to library personnel, faculty, students, and institutional administrators; it should avoid mention of specific skills or sources; and it should focus on outcomes and competencies.

Once library leadership believes it has the beginnings of a plan, it should be shared with and improved by an ever growing group of people. To library personnel, the plan should represent movement from answering simple reference questions, providing point-of-service assistance, and delivering bibliographic instruction to supporting action-based education and teaching electronic information literacy. Within the library, the plan is most likely to succeed if it stresses the goal of information literacy rather than library literacy; if it emphasizes development of life-long information skills; and if it deals with short-term information and reference needs in ways that reduce demands on library personnel.[4]

Classroom faculty, some of whom may never have considered librarians as educators, also need to be brought on board early in the process. The plan for electronic information literacy is most likely to be supported if it complements faculty and administration interests such as improving academic success; increasing student retention; and developing life-long learning skills. To gain acceptance among faculty, the plan will need to assure that faculty members will have opportunities to familiarize themselves with electronic information technology; that the plan assures breadth among student learners; that it will save time for faculty; that it will assess student information abilities; that librarians will work with faculty to create appropriate learning opportunities; and that structured learning experiences will be provided.[5]

Among students, the plan is likely to gain support to the extent that it ensures immediate rewards for the expenditure of time, directly relates to course instruction, and adds market value to the graduate. As library leadership shares the plan, changes and modifications will undoubtedly be made to improve the fit between local user needs and the proposed instruction in electronic information literacy. This is desirable because it increases the probability for success and acceptance. A successful plan will emerge with a clearly defined program and agreed-upon outcomes. It will naturally lead to dynamic action.

Because of the cooperative and interdependent nature of developing electronic information literacy in post-secondary institutions, leadership should emphasize involvement and consultation. Often this is gained through small group meetings involving interested librarians and faculty in a particular area. In these meetings the evolving program can be presented, discussed, and modified, interest can be built, and commitments made. Good leaders will know their subject, invite innovation, encourage enthusiasm, and convert the skeptical.

Library leaders may also decide to hold informal sessions such as electronic information symposia to share the electronic information plan. This would involve librarians, faculty, and administration, and would address information concepts and components and demonstrate applications, preferably from the local institution. Several institutions, e.g., the University of Southern California and Pennsylvania State University, have instituted laboratories where electronic information can be tested and used. Demonstrations and case studies are also important, especially as a consensus becomes apparent, and they are especially vital for sharing views across disciplines and demonstrating agreement. The key is to get others involved.

PRACTICAL AID: CHECKLIST FOR A PLAN

WHAT IS YOUR VISION STATEMENT?

Try to sketch the basic components of your plan for electronic information literacy.

1. What institutional goals do you want to address?
2. What kinds of institutional support can you reasonably expect?
3. What are the educational outcomes and competencies you want to achieve?
4. What are the primary components of a program plan that can result in these outcomes?

Look at your results. Is the plan broad enough to cover the full range of electronic information literacy? Does it emphasize the development of life-long learning skills? Will it improve academic success and increase student retention? Does it address the interests and concerns of librarians? Does it assure coordination with teaching faculty? Does it provide an immediate bang for the buck in terms of student participation? Will it make the student more marketable?

WAYS TO MEASURE NEEDS AND SHARE THE PLAN

- Observation
- Surveys
- Focus Groups
- Symposia
- Outcomes Measures
- Retreats
- Demonstrations
- Informal Discussion

PLANNING AND PUBLICITY

As consensus emerges on the issues of electronic information literacy and the library's role in teaching it, the formal instructional planning process should begin. Similarly, the instructional plan should be appropriate for the end result. The goals should be in full agreement with the values that emerge as part of the needs-assessment process. The objectives should be stated in terms of educational outcomes. The plan should begin with a general statement of needs, plan, action, goals, and objectives. Participation in planning should include all interested parties through a committee or task force.

One of the realities of information literacy is that it is a grass roots movement.[1] While early efforts were often undertaken without much administrative leadership, the growing role of information literacy makes it necessary to integrate overall plans and requirements in a general program plan. The introduction of electronic resources and the concomitant growth in needed resources require additional budgeting and coordinating. Administrators must ensure that the electronic literacy program addresses perceived information needs and is fully articulated with other library programs.

On the other hand, library administration will want to take a light hand in planning to assure broad participation. The administration needs to make clear that it does not wish to dictate what goes on in a classroom or other learning environment. Its job is to support the process and ensure a high-quality outcome.

Librarians, through a committee or some other means, should undertake the bulk of overall planning. Librarians should articulate overall goals, objectives, and activities for the program. A committee can help match specific interests and needs. The committee should discuss alternatives with users and work together to achieve peer consensus on the overall plan.

The overall plan should also identify common professional issues to be incorporated into each course. The extent of information security and privacy should be described for faculty and students. The library's policy on issues, such as copyright and access to remote information, should be described so that administration and instructors can share common expectations in terms of resources. The specific process for developing a new instructional activity or course and the formats for instructional plans should be described to assist instructors in developing new courses.

Once the overall plan is in place, specific instructors will begin to develop syllabi. All specific instruction plans should be reviewed and approved before being implemented. This will involve the establishment of a review committee composed primarily of other instructors; this group will review the proposals for their application to library goals and objectives, academic content, and need. Discipline-specific courses will be shared with the appropriate academic units to secure their endorsement. In most institutions, credit instruction must be submitted for approval at the institution level.

To ensure success, the publicizing of the importance and availability of electronic information literacy training should be given careful attention and financial support. New activities must be described carefully, clearly, and frequently to gain support and participation. Efforts should be made to disseminate information to students, faculty, and departments to encourage their involvement. One-on-one contacts with faculty advisors are particularly recommended as a means of encouraging enrollment in a new and unknown area. Librarians should work closely with faculty to describe and promote the electronic information educational effort.

The library might also run a series of announcements in campus newspapers, and on radio, television, and other broadcasting media. The campus network and electronic mail can be used to distribute information. If the library publishes a newsletter or other handouts, information about instructional programs can be provided. One old adage says that the best kind of advertising is word of mouth. That is certainly true for bibliographic instruction. Several successful courses or other learning experiences will do a great deal to further the library's electronic information literacy goals.

STAFFING

Electronic information literacy brings several staffing issues to most libraries. The first is redesigning work assignments to allow for additional emphasis on instruction. Prospective instructors need to be identified or, more likely, self-identified. Current responsibilities will have to be reviewed and either abandoned or reassigned to undertake instruction. Often, prospective instructors are among the most active and involved personnel in the library, making their reassignment doubly difficult. On a more hopeful note, a person who has completed a great deal of online searching for the last decade may well have both the skills and the time to undertake one or more instructional efforts in electronic information literacy.

Librarians who provide instruction derive many benefits. Because it is an opportunity to exercise creativity, it is one way for an individual to meet personal development needs. It also affords an opportunity to share knowledge with others and to improve human relations skills. Prospective instructors should be knowledgeable in many or most aspects of the topic they intend to teach. While not required to be omniscient, an instructor does have to stay ahead of the class, and in this area there are few textbooks for guidance. Most of all, a prospective instructor should have a desire to teach and to help people learn to master information skills.[6]

Administrators will have to protect and reward creative and outstanding instructors in order to maintain motivation and commitment. Rewards can be both intrinsic and extrinsic. One intrinsic reward is the satisfaction of helping others learn skills and sharing knowledge that the instructor considers important. There is also the recognition by other faculty as a classroom instructor, which, for a librarian, is often a personally validating experience. Extrinsic rewards can include additional compensation for overload activity. Administrators can also provide additional perquisites. If additional income is generated for the library, as much of it as possible should be passed through the system to the instructor for professional benefit through activities such as travel, professional education, and additional technology or materials. If additional resources permit, staff might be hired to replace lost hours at the reference desk. It is also likely that in situations where librarians are already faculty, promotions may come more easily when colleagues in other departments can see a comparable teaching experience on the vita.[7]

Given the dynamic and changing nature of electronic information and literacy education, it is important for management to make training available for instructors on a regular basis. Similar to the instruction proposed in this chapter, such training should involve an opportunity to learn new skills and the opportunity to practice them under existing conditions. Training may address, for example, pedagogical skills, electronic information technology, and information theory. Participants in training should have the opportunity to apply and revise their experience immediately, and evaluate the usefulness of training by pointing to specific improvements in their instructional efforts.[8]

BUDGETING

Library administrators are responsible for applying finite resources in ways that reduce costs and improve effectiveness. This is as true as for teaching electronic information literacy as it is for any other part of the library program. In current conditions of economic stringency throughout higher education, finding these funds can be challenging indeed. Several cost centers are involved. The principal cost is personnel. Most personnel costs are likely to be covered by reassignment from other priorities. Simply put, other things will not be done or will be done less frequently if librarians are to provide personnel support for electronic information literacy. If the library generates student credit-hour funds, the additional funds generated can be used to enrich the course, to reward the instructor, and/or hire replacement personnel. Another way to recover resources is to offer credit instruction through other departments for a fee. An example of this might be charging the Psychology Department for an information and research course for their majors.

There will also be start-up costs. The more mediated the instruction, the more significant the cost. At a minimum, instructors will have to develop lesson plans and materials. At a maximum, an entire course may need to be mediated for distance education. This can involve the production of instructional materials, the development of graphics, scripting for television, electronic mail costs, interlibrary delivery, and other telecommunications. Instructional technologies such as hyperstack can be very staff intensive to develop and maintain. They also involve a significant investment in computer equipment.

Facilities, equipment, and instructional support can also be significant costs. A library may have to install or rent a television studio or computer laboratory. Installing facilities is often very expensive in the beginning. Since these courses often have experiential laboratory activity involving electronic information, equipment and materials are likely to be expensive. Electronic equipment will also have to be available in the library for students and graduates to use. Access to electronic information via the campus network is also desirable. Telecommunications can be costly in that they can involve use of a campus network, Internet, and possibly satellites or ITFS for delivery. Electronic resources, related materials, and reserve readings are likely to change rapidly and to be expensive.[9]

Library administration will have to look at each of these costs carefully to consider what can be funded. The good news is that there are often instruction grants that cover the costs of instructional development and facilities. In addition, if credit instruction is involved, there may be some return for student credit hours developed—if the credit hours come to the library. Outside grants should be actively solicited. For example, Indiana University-Purdue University at Indianapolis recently received a grant to cover the start-up and initial delivery costs of their distance education course on information literacy.

PRACTICAL AID: PREPARE AN INSTRUCTOR ASSIGNMENT AND BUDGET FOR A THREE-CREDIT ELECTRONIC INFORMATION COURSE

Take an existing librarian faculty assignment or job description and draft a revision to teach a three-credit course in an area of library expertise of electronic information. How would you describe this objective? What would define success? What other responsibilities must be maintained? What can be dropped or transferred to others? How will you measure your outcomes?

What instructional resources will you need? What are the costs and benefits of instructor time? What sorts of instructional materials do you require? How large a reserve reading collection is needed? Do you plan a mediated course? If so, what are the costs? Will distance education be involved? If so, what are the costs? What additional facilities or equipment will you require? How many students will you need in your class to make it break even?

ORGANIZING

The need to organize instruction for electronic information literacy has been implied throughout this chapter. Staff organization is as essential for effective instruction as it is for other library operations. As a new area of operation, adjustments in the formal organization may be necessary. These adjustments must fairly reflect the interests of those who plan to teach and those who do not.

Course-level organization must be carried out sensitively, as the instructional process is an intimate one between instructor and student and should be directed by the instructor. In general, library administration should limit its responsibility to assigning time and courses to specific instructors. Peers should review general aspects of course content to assure that they address desired library objectives. Provision must be made for evaluation of results

Increasingly, libraries are adopting matrix or matrix-like formal organizations as they seek to address multiple responsibilities such as electronic information literacy. In a matrix, an individual has different supervisors for different parts of the assignment. In this case, it is likely one librarian will be assigned responsibility for electronic information literacy. This individual will be responsible for instructional activity, instructor assignments, and evaluation. Depending on the size of the library, it is also desirable to develop a critical mass of instructors so that they can share ideas and learn from each other. Sharing experiences and critiquing practice is one of the fastest ways to learn.

Facilities and equipment also need to be organized. The primary decision in this area is whether to buy or build necessary facilities and resources. If the institution has computer laboratories and classrooms, distance education facilities and so forth, it is likely that the library will rent facilities—at least until separate facilities can be economically justified. The same holds true for telecommunications. In the event that there are no appropriate facilities, they will have to be prepared. Space will have to be found, equipment and furniture purchased, and any building modifications made.

The coordinator is responsible for guiding the implementation of the program, obtaining approvals, carrying out ongoing public relations, scheduling and hiring faculty, assigning rooms, and providing support with instructional materials, equipment, and programs. This individual is also responsible for coordinating the evaluation of results.

The coordinator is also responsible for generating enthusiasm for the program and assuring good communications. The best public relations for electronic information literacy is successful instruction. Students will inform their fellows, and these colleagues will enroll in the courses. Communication is essential throughout the institution—up, down, and sideways. Teaching faculty, library personnel, and administration need to receive regular updates and encouragement. Students need to have easy access to their instructors, something electronic mail enhances when the instructor has other duties in addition to teaching.

OUTCOMES

Achieving desired outcomes is the payoff of a quality education program. To the extent that everything goes right, students will learn to be successful information users in the electronic age. They should develop the life-long learning skills needed to define information needs, locate electronic information, critically assess information, synthesize information, and evaluate results.

At NMSU, library instructors have developed achievement assessments for instruction in freshman writing courses. After an hour's instruction and several writing related assignments, 85 percent of students can successfully describe how to find a book and 60 percent a periodical article. The instructors are working on other outcomes measures associated with general education, capstone, and electronic information courses.

Accreditation bodies are committed to using these kinds of outcomes to measure the success of library and information services. The Middle States Association, for example, concludes its library criteria with the statement that " . . . nothing else much matters if the library is not being used." By teaching electronic information literacy, we are likely to create successful, positive, and frequent users of libraries.[10]

CONCLUSION

In the words of a Texas friend, "Managing an electronic information literacy program is akin to herding cats." The field is dynamic and evolves on an hourly basis. Common professional values, appropriately focused on developing skills for life-long learning, are just emerging. Planning must be provisional given the turbulence of the electronic environment, especially the Internet. Necessary skills and abilities of instructors remain only partially defined. Operating funds must be found in a time of financial exigency, often resulting in the reduction or elimination of other activities. Evaluation is critical, but a common body of wisdom regarding what is appropriate has yet to emerge.

Nonetheless, it is an exciting time when a grass roots effort to improve library services is approaching maturity and promises to improve the quality of education and the ability of graduates to succeed in an information society. Administrators can enter these roiling waters confident in the knowledge that they are creating, however haltingly, an important new paradigm for the library profession.

REFERENCES

1. Boisse, Joseph A. and Duane Webster. "Looking Ahead: An Administrative View." In *Bibliographic Instruction: The Second Generation,* edited by Constance A. Mellon. Littleton, CO: Libraries Unlimited, 1987, 45–52.
2. Metz, Ray. "The Impact of Electronic Formats and Campus Networks on University Libraries in the United States." *Computers in Libraries* 10 (May, 1990): 30–31.
3. Coalition for Networked Information. "Program Overview." 1993. Mimeographed.
4. Euster, Joanne R. "Technology and Instruction." In *Bibliographic Instruction: The Second Generation,* edited by Constance A. Mellon. Littleton, CO: Libraries Unlimited, 1987, 53–59.
5. Brevick, Patricia Senn and E. Gordon Gee. *Information Literacy: Revolution in the Library.* New York: Macmillan, 1989.
6. Riggs, Donald A. and A. Gordon Sabine. *Libraries in the 90's.* Phoenix: Oryx, 1990.

7. Townley, Charles T. "Nurturing Library Effectiveness: Leadership for Personnel Development." *Library Administration and Management* 3 (Winter, 1989): 16–20.
8. Lipow, Anne. "Why Training Doesn't Stick: Who Is to Blame." *Library Trends* 38 (Summer, 1989): 62–72.
9. Stabler, Karen Y. "Who's on First, What's on Second: Patterns of Reference Services in Academic Libraries." *Administration and Management* 39 (1993): 13–20.
10. Simmons, Howard L. "Information Literacy and Accreditation: A Middle States Association Perspective." *New Directions in Higher Education* 20 (1992): 15–25.

INDEX